Pedestrian Malls, Streetscapes, and Urban Spaces

Pedestrian Malls,
Streetscapes,
and Urban Spaces

HARVEY M. RUBENSTEIN

John Wiley & Sons, Inc.

New York · Chichester · Brisbane · Toronto · Singapore

Library of Congress Cataloging-in-Publication Data:
Rubenstein, Harvey M.
　　Pedestrian malls, streetscapes, and urban spaces / Harvey M. Rubenstein.
　　　　p.　　cm.
　　Includes bibliographical references and index.
　　ISBN 0-471-54680-1 (cloth : alk. paper)
　　1. Shopping malls—United States.　2. Marketplaces—United States.　3. Plazas—United States.　4. Urban beautification—United States.　I. Title.
　　NA6218.R83　　1992　　　　　　　　　　　　　　92-2897
　　711'.5522—dc20　　　　　　　　　　　　　　　　CIP

Printed in the United States of America

10　9　8　7　6　5　4　3　2　1

To my mother

Preface

It is the purpose of *Pedestrian Malls, Streetscapes, and Urban Spaces* to illustrate how urban spaces evolved historically and led to the development of arcades followed by pedestrian malls, streetscapes, and mixed-use projects with pedestrian-oriented spaces such as festival market places.

This book developed from *Central City Malls* published by John Wiley in 1978. It shows how the various types of pedestrian malls have been modified since their original construction and which types have been the most successful. Originally these malls developed out of the need for renewing downtown shopping areas to compete with suburban shopping centers, to create a new image for a city, to increase retail sales, to strengthen property values, and to promote new investor interest in revitalizing downtown areas. Although some of the pedestrian malls have been very successful or moderately successful, others have failed to meet their original goals.

This book shows how the notion of malls began and the process of developing a mall, including feasibility analysis, planning, and design. This book also reviews the physical factors related to the context of a mall,

streetscape, or urban space such as image and form characteristics.

Design elements and street furnishings are also discussed and are shown photographically. These include items such as paving, sculpture, fountains, lighting, seating, and canopies. The importance of trees in the city for climatic uses, environmental engineering, and architectural and aesthetic values is reviewed with specific examples of trees suitable for the city and the mall or urban space.

To provide in-depth examples of full malls, semimalls, and transit malls, 23 case studies are illustrated for cities of varying size in the United States and Canada. These case studies cover mall description, development strategy, design features, impact on sales, city image, design quality, and changes that have evolved since their construction.

A comparative analysis of the malls follows showing their level of success over the past 5 years and other comparative data on their type, size, cost, funding sources, and benefits. Other spaces that are pedestrian oriented, have shopping facilities, and have mixed uses are discussed in further case studies. These include festival market places and mixed-use projects

with offices, shopping, residential uses, and entertainment facilities. Six examples of various projects in the United States are described and illustrated.

Pedestrian Malls, Streetscapes, and Urban Spaces will be of interest to architects, landscape architects, urban planners, and engineers who are involved in the planning, design, and renovation of pedestrian malls, urban spaces, and mixed-use developments, as well as to students of these professions and to public officials such as mayors, city managers, downtown development directors, city council members, county administrators, and art and planning commission members involved in malls and urban spaces for their cities. In the area of business, members of chambers of commerce, commercial associations, downtown management groups, financiers, developers who promote private investment, as well as students of urban studies and regional science will also find this book to be of value.

Harvey M. Rubenstein
Wilmington, Delaware
June 1992

Contents

6 Plants in the City

7 Pedestrian Mall Case Studies

1

Evolution of Urban Spaces and Pedestrian Malls

View looking down on the Hephaisteion (Temple of Hephaestos) from the Acropolis. The Hephaisteion generated significant influence on the agora, which developed around it.

URBAN SPACES

Introduction

The development of urban spaces, which began with the Greek Marketplace called the agora, grew out of a pedestrian-oriented culture long before the invention of the automobile. Early spaces had facilities related to commerce, government, and places of assembly. During this period of time most patrons of these places also resided in the towns in which the urban spaces were located.

This chapter discusses some of the major spaces one is still able to visit today, such as the Piazza del Campo in Siena, Piazza San Marco in Venice, Piazza di San Pietro and Piazza Navona in Rome, and the Galleria Vittorio Emanuele II in Milan.

These spaces create an image for the city in which they are located; they become a meeting place, and a center for various activities that improve the physical and social environment. In the United States urban plazas do not have the same cultural significance as those in Europe. Recently, however, specialized mixed-use areas such as festival market spaces provide the flavor of some European squares, provide the user with the opportunity to fulfill a specific purpose such as shopping or buying lunch, and also provide the amenities of sculpture, fountains, and well-designed street furnishings. Various types of pedestrian malls or streetscapes often link to these mixed-use areas, particularly in larger cities. Examples of mixed-use urban spaces as well as various types of pedestrian malls will be discussed throughout the book.

The Agora

The Mediterranean climate and the hilly rocky landscape inspired Greek towns and architecture. As commerce and government expanded, the agora became the focus of business, the marketplace, as well as the place of assembly. This was the genesis of modern urban space.

The agora was usually centrally located with principal streets leading to it. It had square or rectangular urban spaces formed by stoas or colonnaded porticos with a facade on one side which provided shelter around the square. Smaller spaces between the buildings led to streets that terminated at the agora. The Greeks stressed human scale and proportion using a ratio of 1.618:1 in much of their architecture, and therefore the size of buildings was designed to relate to people. Greek architecture in its classical form also represents a sense of harmony as an ideal in its buildings and towns.

The open space of the agora was widely used. It was a busy place with a variety of activities and functions where people met, talked, and conducted business and civic activities.

Statues and other sculpture were often placed in the major open space as a focal element. Linked to the agora square, but not facing it, were the assembly hall (ecclesiastron), council hall (bouleuterion), and council chamber (prytaneum).

The Athenian agora, which originated about 420 B.C., was located to the northwest at the foot of the Acropolis, along the route leading to Athens port, Piraeus. From the Acropolis there was a panoramic view looking down to the agora.

The Republican Forum

Where proportion and size of Greek architecture were based on human scale, the Romans used proportions that would harmoniously relate parts of a building, but they were not necessarily related to human scale. Column types called the five orders of columns included the Greek Doric, Ionic, and Corinthian. The Tuscan, a simplified version of the Doric, was added as well as the composite, a more ornate form of Corinthian. The column size, determined by Roman rules of proportion, in turn determined the size of other elements.

This system of proportions was called a module. Roman architecture also utilized the post and lintel used in earlier architecture and combined this with the arch and tunnel vault derived from Mesopotamia. The Romans also advanced the planning of cities with a system of orderly blocks determined by two straight avenues that crossed at right angles, known as a gridiron. The gridiron system of streets enclosed by a wall formed the early colonial town. Both the module and the gridiron system are still used in the planning and design of cities and urban spaces today.

The buildings of the Republican Forum (509–27 B.C.) in Rome represented increasing political power. The Republican Forum, the commercial and governmental center of Rome, began as a marketplace at the base of the hill known as the Capitoline. The buildable area was five or six acres and, at first, buildings were grouped with no apparent relationship to each other except for a narrow axis. As larger buildings were added over a long period of time, the architects began to group the buildings around squares to form

View of the Parthenon at the Acropolis.

The Hephaisteion
(Temple of
Hephaestos) in
Athens, Greece.

The Republican
Forum, Rome, Italy.
(Photograph
courtesy Lynne
Rubenstein.)

urban spaces. Spaces formed by buildings continue to be the principal design approach used in European and American cities.

The Imperial Forum

The concept of the extension of the Forum stressed open space in contrast to the original Republican Forum. Both forums were adjacent to each other. The Imperial Forum (27 B.C.–476 A.D.) had various shaped plazas that were square, rectangular, or semicircular. Each plaza had a colonnade acting as the framework for a focal element, such as a temple, which was located at the terminus of the space. Some individual plazas were lined with colonnades that could also become transitional elements linking various spaces. Single or double rows of columns were used in the ancient Greek manner. All five of the Roman orders of columns were later revived by Rennaissance architects.

MEDIEVAL SPACES

As population increased in size, commerce created the need for market-places. Religious ceremonies, governmental events, and theatrical productions were also held in the plaza. Medieval towns had winding streets with views directed toward nearby buildings or to landmark elements such as the church tower. There was a feeling of orientation in the medieval town, and because of the landmarks, one rarely got lost. Employing this concept recent American pedestrian malls and other urban spaces use landmark elements such as clock towers for orientation. Examples of medieval spaces are discussed in the following.

Piazza del Campo, Siena, Italy

The Piazza del Campo was begun about 1288 and was paved in 1413. It is still one of the finest piazzas in Europe. Located in Siena, an Italian hilltown, the space became and is still used as the gathering area for the whole town. The streets leading into the piazza are narrow, and the open space becomes very dramatic on arrival. It has an ordered spatial structure and a sense of enclosure reinforced by limited sight lines. The main streets are lined with shops, and the entrances are located in relation to the placement of the Mangia Tower. The Gaia (Gaiety) Fountain was added in 1400–1419. Eleven streets radiate out from the square. Use of the existing slope gives the Town Hall its dominant position, and the space has a natural amphitheater effect. The paving pattern has white marble strips in a radial pattern with an infill of deep red brick pavers in a herringbone pattern. The overall space has an organic form and gives the general impression of a shell. The piazza was originally used for horse races, which are still held twice a year at the Palio Festival. It has peripheral uses around it with small shops, restaurants, and cafes. The Town Hall also serves as a museum. The shops, outdoor eating areas, and aesthetic features make it a popular tourist attraction where people gather and relax.

Piazza San Marco, Venice, Italy

One of the most famous outdoor spaces in the world, the Piazza San Marco developed over several hundred years. The Church of San Marco began in 830 as a chapel for the

The Cathedral and Campanile in Siena, Italy act as a landmark. (Photograph courtesy Lynne Rubenstein.)

Doge's Palace, and then in 1000 it was a garden divided by a canal with St. Mark's Basilica on one side. The canal was filled in and the church was reconstructed and enlarged to its present size. It is also one of the most embellished churches in Italy. Alterations were undertaken in 1063 to achieve its current form. The church is the primary focus of the piazza created by the strong axis, but it does not dominate the space. The Doge's Palace was added onto and modified until 1424 when its west facade was built and formed the eastern side of the piazzetta. The Campanille Tower was originally built of timber in 888. It was rebuilt in brick and stone in 1329. The columns and the Lion of San Marco were added in 1189 in the Piazzetta, which faces the Grand Canal, and the statue of St. Theodore was placed in 1329. These columns provide scaling elements adjacent to the Grand Canal. The Piazzetta is essentially a continuation of the open space of the Grand Canal and draws one into the plaza. The space was completed about 1400. The Procurative Veechie was built on the north side of the main piazza for administrative offices in 1480–1517. Following the beginning of this construction the clock tower was built on the western side of the piazza in 1499.

In the sixteenth century an evolution of the space began with the objective of perfecting it. The western

Mangia Tower and Piazza Chapel, which form part of the Palazzo Pubblico (Town Hall) are in perfect harmony with the square in Siena, Italy.

Piazza del Campo with the Gaia Fountain and texture of its brick paving pattern in Siena, Italy. (Photograph courtesy Lynne Rubenstein.)

Piazza San Marco with a view from the Fabrica Nuova toward the church.

side of the Piazzetta was redone with the Libreria, which started in 1536. It was completed in 1584 when the Procuratie Nuove, the new administrative office, was begun on the south side of the main Piazza. The south wall of the big Piazza was torn down for the Procuratie Nuove and moved a few feet further south to detach the Campanile from the original building at its base and thereby make it a free standing element. This work was completed in 1640. The Campanile seems to unify the L-shaped space of the Piazza and Piazzetta. The two above spaces seem to have continuity as one space turns and penetrates or continues into the leg of the other space.

Finally in 1810 the western end of the main Piazza was closed with the construction of the Fabbrica Nuova. This structure permits circulation through at plaza level with a good view of the church at the eastern end of the Piazza.

Both sides of the Piazza and the front of the Libreria have tables and chairs that are used for outdoor dining. The first and second floors of the Procuratie Nuove are used as a museum, as are areas of the Doge's Palace. Overall the square provides an important urban space that serves as a transition between the dense matrix of the city and the openness of the Grand Canal. The space has influenced American design because of its sense of place, focal points, scaling elements such as columns, paving materials, and works of art.

The Piazzetta with the Libreria on the right and a view of the Grand Canal between the columns.

View of the Doges' Palace on the right, Libreria on the left, and campanile from the Grand Canal. The open space of the Piazzetta with the Campanile in the background draws one into the Piazza San Marco, Venice, Italy.

THE RENAISSANCE

The piazzas of the renaissance were carved out of medievel towns and given a monumental scale and form. Sight lines were carefully planned. The renaissance, which began in Italy about 1430 with architect Brunelleschi's dome for the Cathedral of San Lorenzo in Florence for the Medici family, involved the revival of art, literature, and learning in Europe and the increased attention of man's participation as an integral part of the natural world. The renaissance continued until about 1550. An example of renaissance architecture is discussed in the following.

The Campidoglio, Rome, Italy

Capitoline Hill, the location of the Campidoglio, was of religious and political importance in ancient Rome and became the location of the city hall in the middle ages.

The Campidoglio (Capital) was reconstructed by Michelangelo beginning in 1538. It is a link between the early Renaissance in Florence and the Baroque in Rome. The urban space is defined by three buildings that form an enclosed space. The two buildings at the sides of the space are two stories, while the Palazzo del Senatore terminating the space is three stories. A statue of Marcus Aurelius had been placed in the space by Pope Paul III. Michelangelo saw a need for a third building to enclose the space, which at that time had only two buildings. He modulated the uneven top of the hill where he located the Capitoline Museum. Facades of the Conservatoria were redone in 1563–1564 and the Senatorio in 1598–1612. The Capitoline Museum was completed in 1644.

The main part of the plaza is oval shaped, sunken slightly, and has a star-shaped paving pattern. Steps surround the plaza and subtly link it to the surrounding space. The paved area is an important design feature, creating an oval volume of space which strengthens the larger trapezoidal space formed by the three buildings. The square represents a synthesis of nature and culture, providing unity and coherence of design. The major use of the buildings today is for museums.

BAROQUE PERIOD

During the Baroque Period, plazas were created for the display of religious and civic structures such as the Piazza di San Pietro. The spaces could also be renovated, enclosed places such as the Piazza Navona in Rome that was rebuilt with new fountains and sculpture, or they could be piazzas built in new locations as cities expanded, where there was an extension of open space.

Piazza di San Pietro, Rome, Italy

Pope Julius II began the foundation for the new St. Peters in 1506. Work was still proceeding in 1606 during the Baroque Period (late 1590s to 1750) when the long nave was added. The famous piazza was not completed until after the middle seventeenth century. The overall space by Bernini consisted of three areas, each of which was eventually given a specific name. One of these, the Piazza Obliqua, oval Place of St. Peters, was completed about 1660. The piazza slopes slightly toward the

The star-shaped paving pattern of the oval-shaped plaza of the Campidoglio, Rome, Italy. (Photograph courtesy of Lynne Rubenstein.)

obelisk located in its center. The Egyptian obelisk resting on four bronze lions was brought from Heliopolis on the Nile Delta. Flanking the obelisk are two seventeenth-century fountains.

The piazza has a small terracing effect as it rises to the monumental portico. The huge elliptical colonnade at St. Peters was enclosed on two sides by Bernini to make a covered approach to the Vatican. This is reminiscent of the stoa in the Greek agoras. The colonnade has 284 columns, 88 pilasters, and 140 statues.

The Piazza di San Pietro provides a grand approach to an important monument, and it also provides a huge outdoor space for assembly when crowds gather to hear the Pope speak from the Papal Loggia. The square easily holds 300,000 people.

Piazza Navona, Rome, Italy

The Piazza Navona was built during the Baroque period, when Rome was being developed into a shining capital for Christianity. The shape of the piazza, which is curved at one end, exactly duplicates the dimensions of the Stadium of Domitian (240 by 65 m) whose ruins remain beneath the present structure. Great chariot

View of Piazza di San Pietro, Rome, Italy. (Photograph courtesy of Lynne Rubenstein.)

View of Piazza
Obliqua (the oval
space) framed by
the eliptical colon-
nade with the foun-
tain as a focus is
one of the three
areas that comprise
the Piazza di
San Pietro.
(Photography
courtesy of Lynne
Rubenstein.)

View of St.Peters
Church.

races were once held there. The piazza provides a strong sense of enclosure, giving the feeling of being in a great room while also providing a feeling of the overall culture.

The works of two major artists, Borromini and Bernini, are located in the space and placed along the piazza's main axis. Borromini was builder of the church of S. Agnese in 1653–1657. Bernini designed the centrally located fountain of Four Rivers in 1651. The rivers represented are the Ganges, Danube, della Plata, and Nile. The fountain is a synthesis of natural and cultural elements such as water and rocks combined with figurative sculpture and religious symbols. At the south end of the piazza is the fountain of the Moor by Bernini, and at the north end the Neptune by Della Porta, which is a nineteenth century addition. Elevation changes related to the use of Roman stairs are used to bring us close to the ground and give us a sense of belonging to the space.

The overall sense of place, the variety of uses of the buildings forming the piazza, the fountains and sculpture, and the architecture provide reasons why people like to visit the space and insight on how to design spaces for people.

Fountain of Four Rivers by Bernini at Piazza Navona, Rome, Italy. (Photograph courtesy Lynne Rubenstein.)

Fontana del Moro by Bernini with his Four Rivers Fountain beyond and with S. Agnese in the background at Piazza Navona.

Neptune Fountain by Della Porta at Piazza Navona. (Photograph courtesy of Lynne Rubenstein.)

Versailles, France

In Versailles, LeNôtre, a renowned landscape architect, developed his greatest work for Louis XIV of France, with construction starting in 1661 and substantial completion in 1665. Minor changes and additions continued until the death of Louis XIV in 1715. LeNôtre relocated the town, palace, gardens, and park by a system of axes. Versailles has a major east–west axis or sight line that links the centerline of the park from the center of the palace to the horizon or infinity. The other important axis is perpendicular to the above axis that it crosses at the first terrace west of the palace and continues north and south to the face of the building.

In the foreground of the major axis beginning at the palace is a system of terraces with fountains. The overall design links the landscape elements together making the concept understandable to the viewer. The system used at Versailles has had an influence on many projects in various countries. On the townside of the palace three roads radiate toward the palace providing a convergence of vistas at its entrance.

In the eighteenth century during the baroque period the streets in Paris, France focused on the royal palace, whereas in Germany cities such as Karlsruhe, Germany in 1715, revolved around palaces and their related gardens. For example, the overall city of Karlsruhe revolved about and radiated from the Prince's palace. Cities in the United States such as Annapolis, Maryland and Washington, D.C. also use the concept of the axis with radial avenues as a planning and design element.

In the seventeenth century plazas were enclosed isolated spaces, but in the eighteenth century the spaces were more open. An important example of a place that provided open space was the Place de la Concorde, in Paris. The space links the gardens of the Tuileries and the Louvre with the avenue of the Champs-Elysees an important shopping street to connect Paris and the palace at Versailles. The Place de la Concorde started in 1757 and was completed in the early 1770s.

View of Versailles, France.

NINETEENTH-CENTURY SPACES

Regent Street, London, England

John Nash designed Regent Street in London in 1811 to solve functional requirements of the city. The architect developed plans for Regent Street, Regent Park, and Park Crescent. He understood the social, economic, and aesthetic aspects of town planning. Construction proceeded over a 25-year period. Nash created fine buildings around Regent Park and connected it to the city with Regent Avenue. The design concept allowed for normal sized building parcels along the street. Many buildings were designed by Nash, as well as other architects. The street had a well-designed treatment of space without imposing predetermined architecture into the city. Regent street was a mixture of public buildings and commercial offices along with residences, hotels, and a church. The mixed uses of the street were an important concept, which is being used widely today in the United States.

Paris Boulevards

In 1853, Napoleon III put Baron Georges Haussmann in charge of rebuilding Paris. Haussmann concentrated on creating new boulevards, many of which cut through medieval streets but improved the road system and also provided new sites for real estate development. Existing slums were demolished to make room for the new design that created a streetscape with street trees planted along broad boulevards and provided an urban design scheme that gained world renown. The entire boulevard system was planned and constructed within 17 years.

Galleria Vittorio Emanuele II, Milan, Italy

In 1867, when this galleria opened, it was the center of Milan's public society, the place to see and be seen. It is now owned by Milan's municipal government. It was simply the connection of two major generators of pedestrian traffic, the Duomo or cathedral and LaScala, the opera

house. The vertical proportion of the galleria space appears to intensify activity while providing a sense of place. It is not only a place for people to walk but also a place to go for shopping and relaxing in one of the cafes. The galleria or arcade was a commercial use of the street, which lent itself for use as a major urban center. The arcade also evolved in some urban areas because streets were unpleasant places with narrow or nonexistent sidewalks. The concept of the shopping street with separation of pedestrian and vehicular traffic made it more comfortable and safe, anticipating our present shopping malls and pedestrian malls.

World's Columbian Exposition, Chicago, Illinois

The Columbian Exposition of 1893 in Chicago, coordinated by architect Daniel Burnham of Burnham & Root, was to demonstrate the latest technology such as the spanning of large interior spaces with iron trusses. This world's fair began the "City Beautiful" movement across the United States in

View of boulevard in Paris.

which civic centers became the major theme with pedestrian-oriented urban plazas, fountains, gardens, planting, and other street furnishings. The City Beautiful Movement, however, did not solve all the needs of central city commercial areas in the twentieth century. Land took on a new value and building coverage became denser as highrise buildings were developed.

MODERN PEDESTRIAN MALLS

Malls in West Germany

The idea for traffic free zones came from Western Europe. The first renovation of a street into a pedestrian mall occurred in 1926 in Essen.

After World War II pedestrian free zones or malls developed due to increased urban growth, affluence, a large number of cars, and the dense urban fabric with a relatively high residential population.

Cologne, Kassal, and Kiel were the postwar leaders. By 1966 there were over 60 pedestrian malls in West Germany. These malls developed as an ad hoc response to urban congestion in a number of narrow shopping streets. Following this was a boom in pedestrian malls, which led to 214 malls by 1973, 340 malls by 1977, and 800 by the end of the 1980s. The length of the malls also increased from an average of about 250 feet in 1960 to 800 feet in 1973. There were a variety of pedestrian zones. Some had a single pedestrian mall, some

had a series of interlocking streets, squares, etc., and some had unconnected areas.

Eventually, during the 1960s and 1970s pedestrian malls became a major urban planning concern in West Germany. The Federal Government set guidelines in urban policy for state and municipal agencies to follow. It also developed research on malls and passed legislation to create them. Included in the legislation were decisions on creating the malls, their design, and construction. Also, overseeing the evolution and character of the malls was part of the legislation.

In many older urban cities such as Bremen, an oval shaped core originally ringed by a wall had bypass roads constructed to divert traffic around the old city. The central

Galleria Vittorio Emanuele II, Milan, Italy.

Pedestrian Mall,
Hamburg,
Germany.

Sitting area on
Pedestrian Mall,
Hamburg,
Germany.

downtown core area with its public buildings, the cathedral, railroad station, etc. became pedestrian oriented.

In Hamburg, city government improved pedestrian areas by the use of shopping arcades. The arcades were constructed within the redeveloped building blocks. The malls helped to stimulate retail trade in the central business district and reduced automobile traffic congestion. Initially malls had the approval of the public transportation lobby, automobile drivers, environmentalists, and other groups.

In response to the development of suburban shopping centers in Germany in 1971, efforts focused on creating pedestrian malls with clusters of specialty shops, entertainment areas, restaurants, etc. to prevent problems that had hurt shopping areas in the United States. Retailing success became dependent on the variety of shops within the malls and related to a widening gap in rent structure for those on the mall in contrast to those outside it.

By the mid-1970s the decision to build pedestrian malls became contingent on whether they would contribute to upgrading the general environmental quality of an area. As malls progressed into this second stage they began to integrate a wider range of buildings and streetscapes, and include a greater number of the cities shops. This led to the renovation and expansion of the first series of smaller malls.

There are recent proposals for design concepts that provide equal coexistence for both pedestrians and automobiles. Integrated systems of circulation for urban areas that balance the need for local as well as long distance traffic are also being studied.

PEDESTRIAN MALLS IN THE UNITED STATES

In the United States, many cities, beginning with Kalamazoo, began building malls. To date there are approximately 200 pedestrian malls of various types in the United States.

Kalamazoo started with a 2-block mall in 1959. The following year in 1960 a third block was added, and in 1975 the fourth block was completed. All the blocks are closed to traffic. The main retail area with two major department stores is concentrated in the original two blocks and about 35 retail establishments are located on the four-block mall.

The Kalamazoo mall has been moderatley successful over the years and one reason may be that it was developed before the suburban shopping malls were established. It has also been renovated twice, and has provided the downtown with a focal point.

There are about 13,000 people who work in the downtown, and staff from facilities such as the city offices and Bronson Hospital frequent the mall. In addition, other projects have helped the downtown to generate clientele for the mall, especially at lunchtime. A recent $122 million Upjohn research center, as well as a downtown campus of Kalamazoo Community College have been constructed. The shoppers, however, have been mostly from the Upjohn offices. (See Chapter 7 for further discussion of pedestrian malls in the United States and Canada.)

Modern Urban Spaces

The design of urban spaces and pedestrian malls in the United States can draw on European examples. A sense of place with unique character and scale was provided in European piazzas such as Piazza del Campo, Siena, Italy where people can gather and relax. The piazzas have a variety of uses including market areas, civic areas, commerce, religious facilities, and special events such as festivals and horse races. Buildings adjacent to the piazzas were often renovated. In addition there was a sense of containment of the space, which may reinforce one's feelings of protection and security. In recent times since the streets leading to these piazzas were narrow, vehicular traffic has been kept out of these spaces. In the United States, Copley Square in

Boston was recently redesigned to create such a place. A new fountain and comfortable seating are provided. The plaza has been regraded to bring it up to the same elevation as the adjacent peripheral buildings, which adds life to the space.

The architecture of the buildings surrounding European piazzas has provided a sense of scale to the urban environment. The spaces are clearly defined. In the United States the use of buildings with blank facades and those without storefronts along the street such as parking garages interrupt the streetscape and continuity of the block or plaza and must be rethought and where possible reconstructed with street level shops. This was recently done in Santa Monica, California along the facade of the shopping mall facing the 3rd Street Promenade.

American cities need uses and adjacent facilities that add life to outdoor spaces such as shops, cafes, comfortable and convenient sitting areas, quality paving materials with color and texture, works of art such as sculpture and fountains, and street trees for continuity, shade, and seasonal interest.

Providing quality urban spaces including plazas and pedestrian malls encourages use of the city and stimulates a relaxed atmosphere for casual strolling, window shopping, and browsing. To achieve this, convenient and economical parking must also be provided. Parking and transit systems are a key factor in the success of pedestrian malls and urban spaces in American cities. These spaces can be linked to each other for ease of use as has been accomplished in some European cities. Spaces should be inviting, such as Commerce Square in Philadelphia, which encourages people to enter the courtyard where a fountain and outdoor cafes create a place for people to gather, relax, and eat.

The design of festival marketplaces in the United States provided a sense of place for developments such as Faneuil Hall Marketplace in Boston and Harborplace in Baltimore with a variety of shops, restaurants, outdoor cafes, and major pedestrian areas that relate back to the European piazza. The historical quality of the area and the use of materials, graphics, furnishings, and other amenities are inviting to people and these urban spaces have been very successful. The idea of the marketplace with its mixed uses, activities, and amenities relates back to the ancient Greek Agora where the concept for these urban spaces began to develop, and continues to serve the same human needs today.

View of Kalamazoo Mall in its initial form. (Photograph courtesy of City of Kalamazoo.)

View of present
Kalamazoo Mall.
(Photograph
courtesy of City of
Kalamazoo.)

**Children's play
area, Central City
Mall, Williamsport,
Pennsylvania.**

2

Pedestrian Mall Development

Traditionally the word "mall" has meant an area usually lined with shade trees and used as a public walk or promenade. As used today, "mall" denotes a new kind of street or plaza in central city business areas oriented toward pedestrians and served by public transit.

MALL TYPES

The three major types of malls are the full mall, the transit mall, and the semimall. These malls offer a wide variety of designs.

Full Mall

A full mall is obtained by closing a street that was formerly used for vehicular traffic and then improving the pedestrian street or linear plaza with new paving, street trees, street furnishings, and other amenities such as sculpture and fountains. The full mall should provide visual continuity, a special character, and help create an image and sense of place for the downtown.

Transit Mall

A transit mall or transitway is developed by removing automobile and truck traffic on an existing principal retail street and allowing only public transit such as buses and taxis or light rail in the area. The transitway acts as a retail spine or corridor through the downtown. On-site parking is prohibited, walks are widened, and specially designed streetscape treatment is provided to create a unique image for the central city area. The transit mall usually links activities along its route including retail, office, hotel, entertainment, and housing.

Sparks Street Mall, Ottawa, Ontario, Canada. (Photography by Ewald Richter.)

Semimall

In the semimall the amount of traffic and parking is reduced. The expanded pedestrian streetscape areas that result are enhanced with new paving, street trees, street furnishings such as benches, lighting, and signage, and other amenities that provide visual continuity, strengthen the linear character of the street, and create a new image for the downtown. Semimalls are located on primary streets going through major retail areas in center city locations.

MALL DEVELOPMENT

There are many reasons for building one of the pedestrian mall types or streetscapes. The primary one is to revitalize an area of the central business district in a given city in order to increase retail sales, to strengthen property values, to compete with suburban shopping centers, and to encourage private investment by creating a stable environment for retail business. A mall can also create a new image for a city and new opportunities for a mix of uses and for the promotion of retail sales. The

Antique car shows are held in Penn Square, Reading, Pennsylvania.

Children's play area, Central City Pennsylvania.

mall becomes a place in which to improve the quality and variety of downtown activities. It provides a center for exhibits, concerts, fashion shows, flower shows, boat shows, antique car shows, parades, band concerts, arts and crafts festivals, and other events. A mall also provides shaded areas in which to walk, sitting areas in which to relax, sculpture, fountains, outdoor dining areas, and interesting paving and night lighting effects. Quality paving materials and street furnishings should be considered when setting the budget for a mall. A well-planned and designed mall creates an improved physical and social environment for the block or blocks in which it is located and for adjacent areas as well.

Whereas full malls were designed for many of the early projects in the

View of Fulton Street Mall, Fresno, California. (Photograph courtesy of Gruen Associates.)

Trolley stop at transitway, River City Mall, Louisville, Kentucky. (Photograph courtesy of Lynne Rubenstein.)

Hamilton Mall, Allentown, Pennsylvania has been developed as a four-block semimall.

Gay Street Mall paving and street-scape treatment, West Chester, Pennsylvania. (Photograph courtesy of Tetra Tech Richardson.)

1960s and 1970s, semimalls and transit malls are more frequently built today. In some of the early full malls traffic has been reintroduced on some or all of the blocks as the malls have been renovated. Some examples of these are malls in Eugene, Oregon; Muncie, Indiana; Louisville, Kentucky; and Waco, Texas. Transit malls have generally been built in larger cities such as Philadelphia, Pennsylvania; Minneapolis, Minnesota; Denver, Colorado; Portland, Oregon; and Vancouver, British Columbia, Canada.

Downtown retail facilities relied on visibility, on traffic going past the stores. However, in many malls when the automobile traffic was removed, there was not a sufficient volume of pedestrian traffic generated to create a dynamic environment for economic vitality. This required parking and public transit to be provided within easy walking distance of the shops.

It seems that full pedestrian malls or pedestrian free zones have been successful where there are a good diverse mixture of uses with many office workers and/or college students nearby. An example of this is the Wilmington, Delaware Market Street Mall where at noon hundreds of office workers from nearby buildings frequent nearby facilities on the mall for dining, shopping, or just walking or relaxing. From 7th to 10th street the mall has been successful and was renovated in 1986 and 1987. The block from 9th to 10th street is a semimall and has a one way lane of traffic and some parallel parking off to one side of the mall that does not seem to interfere much with pedestrian use. The other three blocks of the mall from 4th street to 7th street were in need of revitalization. These blocks were renovated in 1990 with one lane of traffic and some parking spaces added to form a semimall. It was hoped that the reintroduction of traffic would help give the mall more vitality and greater financial viability (See Chapter 8 on Comparative Analysis of Malls.)

COST

Costs vary greatly in the construction of malls, depending on whether the mall is modest in scope or very comprehensive. In the latter case the complete reconstruction of utility lines and the incorporation of many outstanding amenities may be included in the design. The cost, for example, of reconstructing the three blocks in Wilmington was $750,000 in 1990. Costs of other malls such as major transitways can often range from $500,000 to over a million dollars per block for overall construction including renovation of utility lines, vaults, etc. To achieve the most benefit for the money invested there should obviously be a balance between good design with use of quality materials, and cost. The great interest in revitalizing central city areas and the enthusiasm for the design and construction of malls and streetscapes have also led to increased understanding of the problems that affect downtown areas. For example, when traffic and parking related to pedestrian mall development are analyzed, it usually becomes apparent that in order for a downtown mall to function, adequate parking must be provided within easy walking distance of shopping. Parking and other factors affecting the feasibility of design of a mall are discussed in the following chapter.

Market Street Mall, Wilmington, Delaware is a full mall in the 700 and 800 blocks. These blocks were renovated in 1986 with interlocking concrete pavers and new street furnishings. The mall gets heavily used during lunchtime hours in the blocks that are close to major office buildings. (Photograph courtesy of Tetra Tech Richardson.)

The 600 block of the Market Street Mall in Wilmington with one-way traffic added in 1990. The 400 block and 500 block were also opened to one-way traffic in 1990.

(preceding pages)

View of an informal sitting area at Main Street Mall, Charlottesville, Virginia.

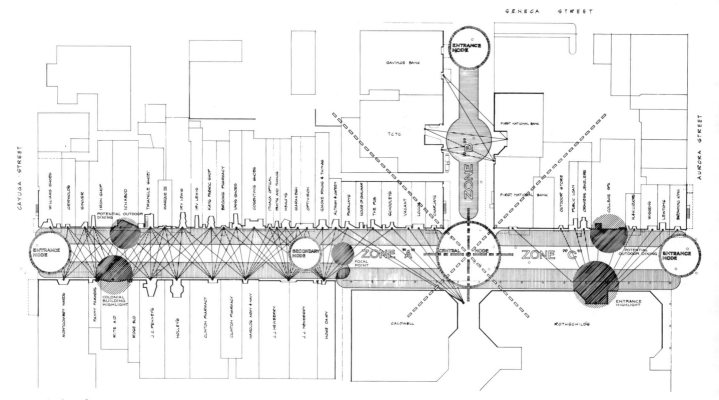

Site analysis, Ithaca Commons. (Photograph courtesy of Anton J. Egner and Associates.)

3

Feasibility Analysis

To determine whether a full mall, transit mall, or semimall can be developed successfully, a feasibility study must be carried out. This study analyzes all the factors—cultural, natural, socioeconomic, funding, political, and legal—that influence the development of a mall as well as the decision as to which type mall is best suited for a particular city or town.

Without a high-quality feasibility analysis, there are insufficient data on which to base a sound decision about building a mall. Upon completion of the feasibility study, the question of whether to build a mall is answered on the basis of the factual information contained in the analysis. If the decision is affirmative, the location, type, length, and cost of the mall are also derived from these data. As the information is inventoried and analyzed, important factors should be illustrated graphically so that they may be easily understood by those reviewing the feasibility report, including the public, whose reactions may influence the outcome of the project.

The following checklist of factors contains many of the items that should be reviewed to determine the feasibility of a proposed mall.

Cultural Factors
1. Traffic.
2. Transit.
3. Parking.
4. Service—trucks, emergency vehicles.
5. Pedestrian circulation—safety, security, origin and destination.
6. Utilities—storm drainage, sewage disposal, electricity, gas, water, steam, telephone.
7. Existing buildings—condition, height, architectural character, vaults.
8. Zoning regulations.

9. Furnishings—signs, lights, street furniture.
10. Maintenance.

Natural Factors
1. Soils.
2. Climate.
3. Topography.
4. Water table.
5. Vegetation.

Socioeconomic Factors
1. Market analysis.
2. Cost–benefit.

Political, Funding, and Legal Factors
1. Approvals.
2. Federal, state, and local funding.
3. State and city laws.

CULTURAL FACTORS

Traffic

When a mall is proposed, the first question that usually arises is whether adjacent streets can handle the additional traffic. In some downtown areas these streets may already be overloaded with traffic. To determine the viability of placing a mall in a specific block or blocks, it is necessary to measure the actual traffic volumes already utilizing the street or streets involved. This includes gathering data on the following:

1. Origin and destination of vehicles.
2. Average daily traffic volumes.
3. Peak hour traffic volumes—morning and afternoon.
4. Turning movement counts at all intersections.

"Origin and destination" denotes where traffic is coming from and where it is going. This information, as well as trip purpose, is obtained from interviews. To accomplish this, a cordon is circumscribed around the central business district (CBD) and traffic is counted entering and leaving. The survey on trip purpose is also carried out in this area. Once the desired traffic data for the proposed street location of the mall are obtained, a similar evaluation must be made for adjacent streets that would receive the diverted traffic. The data for the diverted traffic are then superimposed

over the streets designated to receive it. If the data provided by the traffic study determine that in the present circulation system adjacent streets cannot handle the additional traffic, there may be alternatives. In some cases, for example, a revised one-way street system will eliminate turning movement at intersections, thereby increasing capacity during peak hours by simplifying the traffic signalization. Timing the traffic signals so that they are well coordinated also improves capacity. A bypass route also does much to resolve traffic congestion, although this may be a long-term alternative. The matter of developing a mall often raises further questions about the overall downtown circulation plan. The mall may therefore act as a catalyst to improve the overall downtown traffic pattern. This was the case in Fresno, California, where a loop was provided around the entire downtown core and freeway routes were located 20 years ahead of the proposed construction dates. Proposing changes to the existing downtown traffic scheme is likely to elicit some public criticism. Usually, however, these complaints will cease after the mall is completed and the vehicular circulation problems are improved.

In some communities closing a block to traffic has been attempted as a test to see whether the adjacent blocks can handle additional traffic. This trial procedure has sometimes had positive results, as in the Sparks Street Mall in Ottawa, Canada (see p. 156). It does not work as well, however, if no other changes have been made to the block for improving traffic flow, and no amenities have been added. This was the case with the Hamilton Mall in Allentown, Pennsylvania (see p. 169), where a full mall had been desired at first. The trial results in unfavorable publicity for the mall idea if adjacent streets become overloaded, if on-street parking spaces are removed without other provisions for parking, and if bus routing is interrupted.

Traffic studies should be carried out under the direction of a qualified traffic engineer to ensure accuracy and comprehension. If a community has such an engineer on its staff, he or she will be able to coordinate and analyze the data; if not, a consultant should be retained.

Public Transit

Bus routes are another important area for study. Developing a full mall on a major block or blocks presupposes moving bus stops to other streets.

Changing a two-way street system to a one-way system may mean moving bus stops to the other side of the street. It may also involve relocating bus shelters or developing new ones. Bus stops in the vicinity of the proposed mall should therefore be inventoried.

Taxi service will also be affected if a full mall is developed. Taxi stands or drop-off areas may have to be developed on adjacent streets. The impact of the mall in terms of traffic and transit must therefore be studied in its overall context, with consideration given to other streets in the area. These streets should be reviewed for parking, bus stops, taxi stands, and truck loading zones.

Parking

When a full mall or transit mall is constructed, parking spaces are removed. These spaces are generally also reduced or removed for a semi-mall. With parking in short supply in many downtown areas, the parking spaces must be relocated or added in areas within convenient walking distance of the mall. The mall may well generate a need for additional parking, or parking may have been inadequate even before the study was made.

One of the reasons for the success of the suburban shopping mall is the convenient free parking. If a downtown mall is to compete, convenient low cost parking is essential.

The city of Ithaca, New York, provides 45 minutes of free parking adjacent to the Ithaca Commons (see p. 141). Eugene, Oregon, provides unlimited free parking for shoppers.

If, in the downtown plan, it is determined that surface parking and curb parking are not adequate, multilevel parking structures should be considered. The economic feasibility of a parking structure is based on how much of the construction cost must be allocated for amortization and interest. At $20,000 to $22,000 per parking space, it takes about $8.00 per day per space just to break even. This means that the space will not carry itself on $0.50 per hour, or even $1.00 per hour in some cases. Revenue projections should carefully consider parking rate structure to obtain a realistic picture of income. All factors related to the design of the parking facilities, such as capacity, access, and layout, should be reviewed before financing is arranged. To help pay for a parking structure, and to keep parking rates in the new structure low, a form of financial assistance such as rental income from shops at street level, or balancing expenses by means of surface lots or curb meters already in existence, may be necessary.

Parking should be located in such a way as to minimize walking distance to the mall. One way to accomplish this is to develop parking lots or garages on streets parallel to the mall. Parking garages may also be built with pedestrian walkways bridging streets and leading directly into the mall. Sometimes parking is also located behind existing stores on the mall, and may be connected to the mall by walkways between buildings or linked directly to department stores.

Service and Emergency Access

In the development of a full mall, accessibility for service is a major functional consideration. Service vehicles include trucks for deliveries, shipments, and trash removal, and emergency vehicles such as ambulances, police cars, and fire trucks. When a block is closed to cars and buses, trucks are also barred. Is there an alternative means of access so that buildings can be served from alleys, back streets, or special loading zones?

A building-by-building survey of how services are currently handled must be made in order to review the feasibility of servicing the businesses when a mall is in existence. This study includes deliveries, shipments, and trash removal. If the survey shows that servicing the buildings from service cores or alleys is not practical, it may be necessary to allow service vehicles on the mall for specified periods, such as 7:00 P.M. to 10:00 A.M. An alternative method may be to develop a service lane through the mall.

Transit stops, on-street parking, and truck loading are inventoried for a mall feasibility study for Scranton, Pennsylvania. (Photograph courtesy of Bellante, Clauss, Miller and Nolan.)

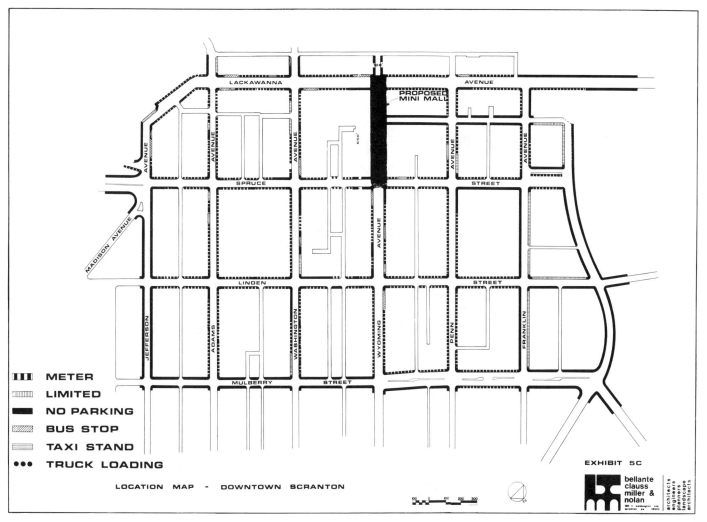

LOCATION MAP - DOWNTOWN SCRANTON

III METER
LIMITED
NO PARKING
BUS STOP
TAXI STAND
••• TRUCK LOADING

EXHIBIT 5C

bellante
clauss
miller &
nolan

architects
engineers
planners
landscape
architects

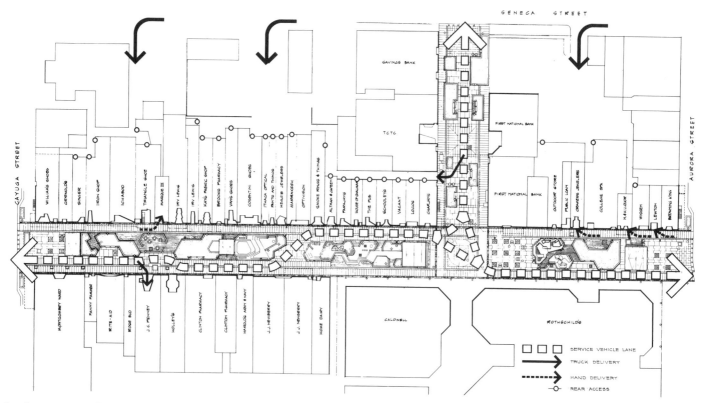

GENECA STREET

SERVICE VEHICLE LANE
TRUCK DELIVERY
HAND DELIVERY
REAR ACCESS

Service areas study, Ithaca Commons. (Photograph courtesy of Anton J. Egner and Associates.)

A service lane is used in Penn Square, Reading, Pennsylvania.

Room must also be provided for emergency vehicles such as police cars, ambulances, and fire fighting equipment. Usually a 15-foot-wide open space or lane that is part of the pedestrian area will be adequate. Meetings with local police and fire companies will help determine these functional requirements. For example, in Ithaca, New York, the fire department built a model of the mall to study access for fire-fighting vehicles and equipment suitability.

Pedestrian Circulation

The primary objectives of improved pedestrian circulation are safety, security, convenience, continuity, coherence, comfort, and aesthetics. Fulfilling one of these objectives generally increases the opportunities for meeting or improving the others. Ease of pedestrian circulation with safety from vehicular conflict is one of the primary purposes and benefits of developing central city malls.

Two methods of reducing conflicts between pedestrians and vehicles are time separation and space separation. Traffic signals are a mechanism for providing time separation. There are still conflicts, however, because of vehicular turning movements. In some cities an "all walk" sequence where pedestrians have exclusive crossing rights is used at busy downtown intersections. This system generally produces greater numbers of people waiting at corners to cross the street than would otherwise be the case.

Space separation is achieved by closing streets to vehicles and creating malls. The full mall acts as a pedestrian plaza, and people may walk freely between the two sides of the space. Space separation can also be achieved by the use of underpasses or overpasses; if these are not within the direct line of pedestrian traffic, however, they may not be fully used because of the inconvenience of a longer walking distance. This has happened on the Fort Street Mall in Honolulu, Hawaii (see p. 138).

The inventory of the proposed mall area should include the dimensions of each street and sidewalk. Also included should be information on all traffic regulations, signs, signal locations, signal cycle length, and traffic (volumes from the traffic survey). The sidewalk survey should show the locations and dimensions of buildings and the transit system locations or entrances.

The inventory should also examine pedestrian trips, including their

Space separation is achieved by the use of an underpass at Vallingby, Sweden.

origins and destinations, purposes, time of day, and volume. For large pedestrian networks this information is difficult to obtain, and special methods must be used. These methods include cordon counts, origin and destination surveys, pedestrian density surveys by aerial photographs, and mathematical modeling.

Trip Purpose and Characteristics

Most pedestrian trips are relatively short, only a few blocks, because pedestrians seek parking spaces within 600 feet of their destinations. If the purposes and types of pedestrian trips are understood, better pedestrian facilities can be developed. Pedestrian trip purpose is closely related to the type of land use associated with trip origin or destination. The number of trips attracted or generated by an activity depends on its size and type. For example, large retail stores will attract more trips than small retail stores.

Pedestrian trips are categorized into three major types: (1) terminal trips, (2) functional trips, and (3) recreational trips.

TERMINAL TRIPS are made to and from home or points associated with transportation mode areas: parking lots, bus stops, and transportation stations. *FUNCTIONAL TRIPS* are made to carry out a specific function, such as business trips related to work or personal business trips involving shopping, dining, or going to a doctor's office. *RECREATIONAL TRIPS* are made for purposes related to leisure time. These include going to the theatre, concerts, and sporting events, as well as social activities in which walking is one of the primary purposes.

NODES

In the pedestrian network there are two basic types of nodes. One is the origin and destination (node) of the walking trip. Nodes are centers of pedestrian activity or points of con-

centration. These are classified as primary or terminal nodes and secondary or activity nodes.

PRIMARY NODES are associated with mode transfer where walking trips begin and end, such as parking areas and transit stops.

SECONDARY NODES are other locations that attract trips from primary nodes as well as from other secondary nodes, such as offices, stores, and restaurants.

In summary, various types of studies must be carried out to determine whether there are problems related to pedestrian circulation in a given area. For example, the analysis may show that large numbers of pedestrians use the particular area designated for a mall, and that certain sidewalk areas must be significantly widened to accommodate the pedestrian traffic. The study may also demonstrate that space separation is needed to solve problems of pedestrian–vehicular conflict. This is an important consideration in determining the overall

Existing building survey, Ithaca Commons. (Photograph courtesy of Anton J. Egner and Associates.)

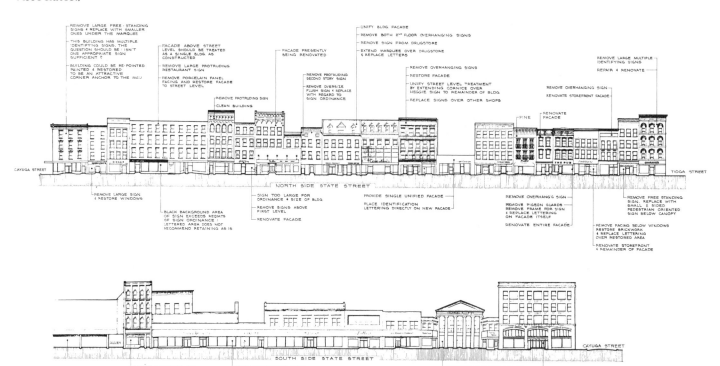

feasibility of the mall and its type—whether it should be a full, a semi, or a transit mall.

Utilities

In considering mall development, it is necessary to review the existing utilities and to plan for upgrading the systems when necessary. These utilities include storm water drainage, sewage disposal, electricity, gas, steam, potable water, and telephone. If a street has outdated utility lines, such as combined sanitary and storm water systems, the lines should be separated while the block or blocks are being reconstructed. A new utility core through the entire block may be desirable. If electric lines to existing light poles are still above ground, it may be possible to place new lines below grade.

The costs for revamping the utility system must be carefully evaluated because a major share of the project cost may be absorbed by these lines,

which are invisible on the surface. In some malls the utilities have cost as much as one-third to two-thirds of the total construction budget.

Even if existing utilities are in good condition, their locations must be carefully considered so that the lines can be maintained when necessary with as little disruption as possible to mall activities. A very detailed topographic survey is needed, locating all of the existing facilities and giving rim and invert elevations of manholes and catch basins, as well as elevations at the entrances to all buildings and at intersections, service roads, and any other critical places. The city engineer can provide information on sizes of lines. This information should be verified by the utility companies. Perhaps these companies have planned to upgrade their lines and would be willing to do the work in conjunction with the development of the mall. Older cities often have some antiquated systems, such as steam lines for heating parts of a downtown

area, or perhaps combined sanitary and storm lines. These lines may need work because of their age. The mall development provides an opportunity to separate the storm water lines from the sanitary lines, to build vaults so that the lines may be easily serviced in the future, or to do other needed work. In any case the utility systems must be carefully reviewed, along with the soils beneath the mall.

Existing Buildings

Existing buildings in the area of the proposed mall must be carefully surveyed as to their condition, height, front footage, and architectural character. Architectural character includes the building facade, color, texture, materials, window type, and roof style. Some of these buildings may have basement vaults that project beneath existing sidewalks. The size, location, and structural condition of each vault must be determined. How much room is there between existing

Vault plan, Ithaca Commons. (Photograph courtesy of Anton J. Egner and Associates.)

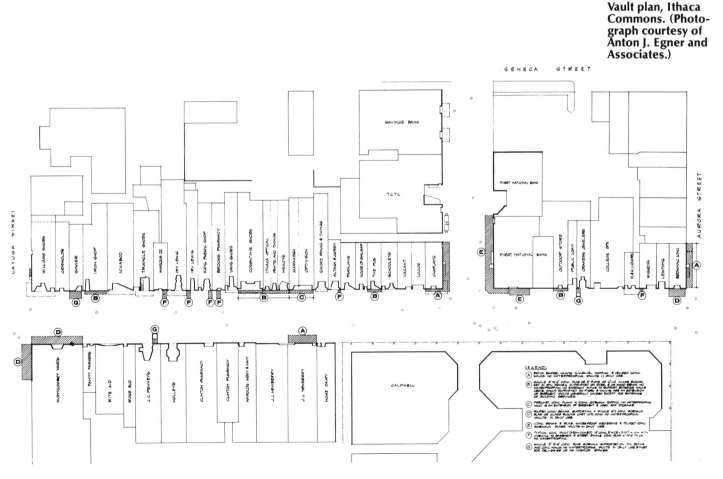

vaults and the finished grade of the existing sidewalks? Will the vaults have to be waterproofed if new sidewalks are installed? Also, will the vaults be able to bear additional weight if necessary, or must they be rebuilt?

If a particular building is in bad condition, costs would be incurred by having it torn down in order to build the mall. Programs may sometimes be developed concurrently with the mall construction to help merchants finance new facades or carry out other rehabilitation or renovation of their buildings. This has been done for several malls, such as Oldtown Mall in Baltimore (see p. 112).

Reviewing these factors for several different vicinities that have some potential for a downtown mall may show the condition of buildings in a particular area to be a significant factor.

Street Furnishings

Elements on existing sidewalks or overhanging sidewalks are called street furnishings. These include signs, lights, traffic signals, parking meters, fire hydrants, benches, and flower pots.

These elements must be inventoried in the overall street context. A new sign ordinance may be necessary to improve the aesthetics of the downtown. Elements such as fire hydrants or light poles may have to be relocated if a mall is developed. Traffic signals of the older type, hanging across streets by overhead wires, should be replaced by new modular units that include the traffic signals, pedestrian walk signals, and night lighting.

Maintenance

Once a mall has been constructed, it must be maintained. Maintenance consists of sweeping the mall, removing trash, replacing light bulbs, removing snow in many regions, and watering, spraying, and fertilizing trees and shrubs, as well as replacing broken items and perhaps planting flowers in the spring and putting up Christmas decorations in the fall. Can the proposed mall be designed so that it can be well maintained at a reasonable cost? Durable materials and good detailing and construction methods help keep maintenance costs down.

Continuous maintenance will be necessary and must be programmed into the overall cost of the mall. Who will carry out the maintenance? In many areas, cities will take care of this function. Often, however, supplemental maintenance is necessary. If state law permits assessment of property owners for this purpose, the problem may be solved; if not, an association to manage this service must be formed.

This canopy provides some weather protection in Wilkes-Barre, Pennsylvania.

NATURAL FACTORS

Natural factors such as the climate, topography, soils, water table, and vegetation of a proposed area must also be reviewed.

Climate

Temperature, humidity, precipitation, and wind are important considerations in the design of a mall. If the mall is located in an area with severe climate—either hot or cold, or involving much precipitation—covered walkways may be desirable. This type of feature can be quite expensive, but it has been used in the design of several malls. Microclimate or variation in local climate will also have an important impact on the location of elements within a mall. Shade trees, for example, could be planted in the areas of the mall having the most exposure to the sun. Since people enjoy sitting in shaded areas that provide protection from the sun, benches might be added in these areas. If a fountain is a feature of the mall, having the sunlight reflect off the water would be an important consideration in its location. Climate is also important in the design of construction details and in the maintenance of a mall. In cold climates, footings for various elements must be below the frost level. Also, consideration must be given to the types of paving materials used in the construction of the mall. Will the paving materials allow water to percolate down to the roots of trees, and will the use of salt during winter months have a detrimental effect on paving materials or planted areas? These factors are very important in the design of the mall.

Soils and Water Table

Soils must be studied to see whether there is any limitation on the type of facilities to be placed on the mall. In addition, the soil study will consider placement of utility lines and foundations. The water table must also be explored in relation to subsurface conditions. In areas with special situations, such as a city with old mine shafts beneath it, special consultants may be necessary to review possible problems.

Topography

The topography of an area often has a great influence on the location and design of a mall. The topography will also influence the location of activity areas. In some malls topography has been used to create unique effects.

The topography of the existing area must be studied very carefully, and a comprehensive topographic survey must be carried out so that all critical elevations on a block may be reviewed when the mall is in the design stage. This review should point out problems related to dealing with water runoff, saving existing trees, and meeting grades at entrances to buildings.

Vegetation

What types of trees, if any, exist where the proposed mall is to be built? Will planting trees in a particular block encounter any problems, such as vaults located under the present sidewalks? The uses of vegetation are discussed in Chapter 6.

SOCIOECONOMIC FACTORS

A study of the community and its social and economic structure is important in determining the feasibility of a mall.

Topography has been used to an advantage at Essex Mall, Salem, Massachusetts.

Business in the downtown area must be of sufficient regional potential to justify the cost of a mall. The level of business should be projected to increase or at least hold the line. If this is not the case, the feasibility of the mall is in doubt.

The size and costs of the mall must be realistic in relation to the volume of business taking place on it or adjacent to it, and also in relation to the property values on or near it.

Market Analysis

Socioeconomic feasibility is based on a market analysis and projection. The analysis should be carried out by experienced professionals and should cover the trade area, population characteristics, buying power, and competition.

TRADE AREA

The trade area is the region that supplies major continuing patronage for a business area. It includes the primary trade area, within a 5-minute drive or a radius of about 1.5 miles; the secondary trade area, within a 15- to 20-minute drive or 3- to 5-mile radius; and the tertiary trade area, within a 25-minute drive or 7- to 8-mile radius. The survey of the trade area should consider traffic modes, access to the mall, and location of competitive facilities.

POPULATION

The population characteristics within the trade area must be studied to identify the potential user of the mall. These characteristics include population number, population growth, and factors such as income level, age, and family size. This information is obtained from census data.

SOCIAL CONCERNS

Other social factors to be identified, in addition to who the user or urban consumer is, are the activities, events, and programs that he or she desires to be programmed into the design and operation of a mall. Downtown areas are busy places providing a variety of activities, features, and functions. These elements, properly located, will help to generate an improved social environment in the downtown, which in turn will lead to improved economic patterns.

Public opinion surveys can establish what new activities, uses, and features would be desirable in a mall. Objectives can then be established for space requirements for these elements when the mall is designed. Promotional events such as puppet shows, car shows, boat shows, fashion shows, parades, art exhibits, craft exhibits, fund raising events, and special programs such as band concerts can be held. Other uses relate to vendors, outdoor restaurants, information booths, or related items that add to the particular sense of a place. Feature elements include items such as fountains, sculpture, children's playgrounds, and clock towers.

Upon completion of the mall, promotion should be actively started to attract people. The promotion can be aimed at increased pedestrian traffic, tourists, young people, senior citizens, and families. An ongoing promotion coordinator may be hired to schedule a wide variety of events to help create interest in the mall and draw people to it.

PURCHASING POWER

Income levels within the trade area are important in showing the number of dollars available in relation to expenditures for categories of goods and services such as food, should be formulated so that benefits can be measured. Economic benefits can be projected from the market analysis data. Enough data are generally available to determine factors such as projected increase in retail sales, tax revenue, and property taxes, increase in the market value of improvements, and increase in the number of jobs. Other potential benefits are higher land values, greater numbers of customers, and heavier use of public transit. Social and community benefits may be evaluated by means of opinion surveys with such questions as, "Will the mall help to upgrade existing community facilities, provide for new ones, or increase open space?" Functional benefits include such things as improving downtown traffic, service, safety, and security. Some examples of environmental benefits are control of air pollution, improvement of aesthetic quality, and preservation of historic buildings.

A cost–benefit analysis can bring many favorable factors to the public's attention and be instrumental in arousing community support for building a mall.

POLITICAL, FUNDING, AND LEGAL FACTORS

A feasibility study is more than a review of traffic, parking, and market analysis; it is a public relations document. It must be a sound document competently done by professionals so that it can be used as a selling tool.

Political Factors

An important question is whether a mall is politically feasible. Can the votes and approvals needed to make the mall a reality be obtained? Who has the final decision-making power on closing a street or reducing the number of parking spaces for a semimall—the mayor, city council, or state? Those who advocate building a mall should find out which groups or individuals may present problems and then meet with them to discuss the benefits of the mall and at least to neutralize their doubts so that they will not hinder the project. The feasibility study should help answer all the questions that may arise about the mall and should be made available to the public. Parts of the study may be published in the local newspapers, and copies placed in the library.

Obtaining an early commitment to the project and support from the business community, property owners, newspapers, politicians, and municipal administrators is helpful, as is establishing a downtown study committee with representatives from all the above groups to keep the project moving and to act as spokesmen for it.

Funding

If the feasibility analysis demonstrates that the project is viable, funding can be obtained. Funding from as many sources as possible is desirable, so that each can make a contribution to the overall project.

Several types of funding are available for malls. The federal government gives Community Development Program grants to many cities. A portion of these funds may be allotted to a mall.

The Department of Commerce, Economic Development Administration, is another possible source of funds. It makes money available to provide jobs in project areas under its Public Works Program. The Urban Mass Transportation Administration also makes grants for projects related to a coordinated transportation system. This agency has funded projects such as the Chestnut Street Transitway in Philadelphia and the Portland Transit Mall.

Funding by state community affairs departments is also possible in some areas. The Hamilton Mall in Allentown, Pennsylvania, was partially funded in this way. Sometimes special assessment districts are established. Many states have legislation that permits assessment on properties abutting or adjoining a mall. All commercial and retail establishments should be included in the districts. Contributions to the development should be mandatory rather than voluntary. The assessment district may be based on front footage or gross square footage. A percentage of construction cost and maintenance can be financed by this method. Cities issue bonds, and properties in the assessment district pay off the interest and principal. Assessments can also be used to match funds from outside sources.

Legal Factors

State law must be researched to see what is possible under the laws on assessment. If legislation does not exist on assessment, a bill can be introduced into the state legislature. The state highway department can advise whether there are legal problems in closing or modifying a city street that is also a state route. In most cities an ordinance must be passed by the city council and the mayor in order to narrow an existing city street or to close a street completely to create a full mall. In some cases a bill may have to be enacted by a state legislature in order to establish a mall.

In the state of Washington, the Edmonds City Council resolved to have a pedestrian mall and then found that it was legally impossible. Through the Association of Washington Cities, Edmonds avoided litigation when the state legislature approved a bill to create a mall.

(preceding pages)

View of Harbor-place, Baltimore, Maryland.

Overall context of Ithaca Commons, with study of bus routes. (Photograph courtesy of Anton J. Egner and Associates.)

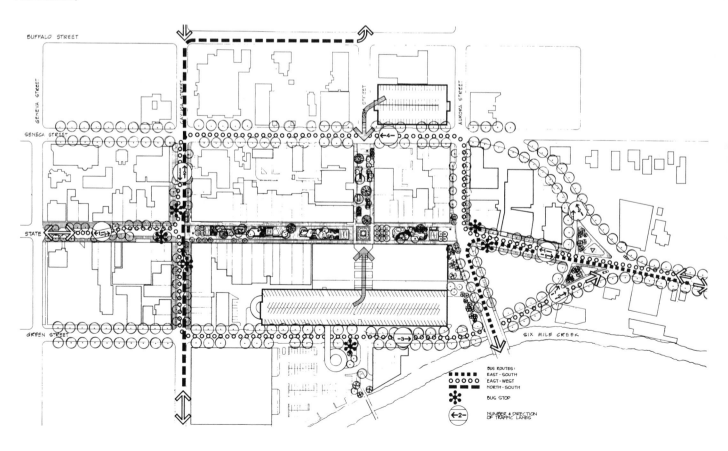

4

Context and Form Characteristics

As a mall or urban plaza is developed, it should be viewed in the context of the entire downtown. This means that in studying the physical relationships of a mall or plaza to the central city and in strengthening the project's identity or image, one must go beyond the immediate environment of the mall, streetscape, or urban space and examine the larger central city context.

CONTEXT

Central City Image

The image of a central city is based on its shape, color, texture, arrangement, and sensory quality, all of which give the observer clues to its identity and structure.

Image has been classified into five elements, which may be isolated for closer study. These elements are paths, nodes, edges, districts, and landmarks. They are described as follows.

Paths

Paths are the circulation routes or lines along which people move. They are the streets, walks, and transit and rail lines.

Nodes

Nodes are centers of activity into which one can enter. They are junctions or crossings of paths, or points of concentration such as plazas. They may also be places of transportation mode activity such as railroad, bus, or subway stations.

Edges

Edges are linear boundaries that distinguish one area or region from

Path: Riverwalk tourist area in San Antonio, Texas.

Node: Spanish Steps (Piazza di Spagna) with Baraccia Fountain in the foreground, Rome, Italy.

another. An edge may be a river, which is a strong feature in outlining the boundary of a city, or it may be a path such as an elevated roadway, or a row of buildings forming the outline for an area.

Districts

Districts are medium to large parts of a city that have common distinguishing characteristics. They are identifiable from the inside and can be used for exterior reference if viewed from the outside. The more easily they can be seen from a distance, the more useful they are in guiding direction. A district is an area of a city with which people identify and which generally has a name, such as North Side, East End, or Hill Section.

Landmarks

A landmark is a physical object such as a building, tower, sign, dome, mountain, or hill. Landmarks may vary in scale, may be close or distant, and sometimes may be seen only from specific approaches, as from the junction along a path. Landmarks aid in the identification of points of choice and direction. A landmark may be a place known to observers that give them cues so that they may make a choice, for example, as to which turn in a road junction to take. Distant landmarks also aid in maintaining direction. Paths, nodes, edges, and landmarks work in conjunction with each other to form the structure of the central city. Of these elements, paths are the most important in pro-

viding order. Major paths should have their own identities. Each should have some quality that distinguishes it from the surrounding network. This can be spatial quality, a special paving pattern, a unique texture of material on walks or building facades, or a particular lighting pattern, planting design, or activity that gives continuity to the path.

In any existing central city area where a mall may be built, there is an image even if it is cluttered and not apparent. In developing a mall the challenge lies in reshaping an existing street environment and strengthening its image. A mall can therefore enhance the image of the central city by helping to clarify its structure and identity.

Edge: Walk and steps along Riverfront Park in Cincinnati, Ohio, form a strong edge.

47

Landmark: This triangular space frame structure at the Louvre Museum, Paris acts as a landmark element. (Photograph courtesy of Lynne Rubenstein.)

Inventory and Analysis

An inventory and analysis must be made of existing physical elements in the vicinity of the mall. Strong features must be identified and reinforced, while weak elements are removed or strengthened. For example, a city may have unsightly overhead wiring for its street lighting. These wires should be placed underground.

Perhaps a particular building is rundown and needs to be rehabilitated. Graphic maps, drawings, and/or diagrams should be made to illustrate these factors or conditions. In an inventory of central city features related to the mall's image, items of visual pollution become evident. In many older cities there is a clutter of street furnishings, such as traffic signals, poles, signs, and parking meters.

The analysis of physical factors can also reveal which, if any, street furnishings are causing visual pollution. At the urban scale the details of elements in the street may be as important as buildings in determining the aesthetic quality of a city. It is therefore most important to review the elements that provide form for the city, identifying the items that give continuity to the downtown context and restructuring other items to improve visual quality. The following discussion reviews the form characteristics that provide design quality. This should lead to improved understanding of the design factors and form characteristics with which architects and landscape architects must be familiar in order to relate a mall or urban space to an existing urban context.

FORM CHARACTERISTICS

The following characteristics should be considered in giving design or aesthetic quality to urban space.

Figure-Ground

Figure-ground is the contrast of an object to the ground. An element appears as a figure if it stands out

Clutter of overhead wiring.

This Milles Sculpture in Stockholm, Sweden stands out as a figure against the sky acting as ground.

against undisturbed ground. For example, trees are the figures that stand out against the sky acting as ground. Other vertical elements on a mall or plaza, such as lights, can stand out as figures in contrast to buildings. Such contrast gives an object clarity and identity.

Continuity

Continuity is provided by a series of coherent parts. The parts may be related by keeping a common scale, form, texture, or color for a space or area. For example, use of brick pavers of a particular color on a mall or plaza gives continuity to the paving.

Sequence

Sequence is continuity in the perception of space or objects arranged to provide a succession of visual change. It may create motion or mood, or give direction. One space in a sequence may create mood by having a bosque of trees or an overhead structure to provide enclosure, while the following space is open.

Repetition

Repetition is the simplest kind of sequence. It may involve shape, color, or texture, and only a single part need be repeated. For example, a particular type of street light could be selected and repeated throughout a mall or streetscape area or the overall central city.

Rhythm

Rhythm is a sequence of repetitive elements interrupted at specific intervals. Rhythm can be incorporated into a paving pattern by creating a design with a change from brick to concrete bands at specific intervals.

Size and Scale

The size of an object or space is relative and depends on the distance of the object from the observer. Scale denotes relative size and is based on the height of an average observer, 5 feet 9 inches. The scale of space, therefore, is related to the observer himself. In viewing a building, the eye has an angle of vision of about 27 degrees. To see a whole building at this angle, one must be at a distance that equals twice the building height. In relating outdoor space to buildings there is a sense of balance when a space has a width equal to the height of the building or twice the building height. Once the space is larger than four times the height of the building, interaction between building and space dissipates. In a space 80 × 80 feet in size, people can still identify each other. As spaces go beyond about 150 × 200 feet in size, it is difficult to retain the feeling of intimacy of smaller spaces.

Shape

Shape gives quality to the relative form of an object. What is the shape or form of a space? Is it rectilinear, curvilinear, or triangular?

Proportion

Proportion is the ratio of height to width to length. Ratios have been developed to achieve a series of dimensions that are related to each other and to a largest size. The Greeks built their temples with a length:width ratio of 1.618:1. Simple ratios such as 1:1, 1:2, 2:3, 3:4, and 3:5 are perceived and used to design architectural elements.

Hierarchy

Hierarchy is a system used to rank sizes or colors. Hierarchy can be applied to rank the sizes of elements in a paving pattern or to give prom-

Continuity of paving can be achieved by the use of a paving material such as brick or concrete.

inence to an area around a sculpture or fountain by changing the size or color of the paving materials.

Dominance

Dominance denotes importance over other parts because of having the largest size or the most prominent position. In a mall or plaza there may be a dominant space or area containing a special activity or focal element.

Texture and Pattern

When one cannot determine the size and shape of individual parts as they form a continuous surface, there is texture. When one can differentiate the parts forming a whole, there is a pattern. Texture can be provided by the type of materials used or by surface treatment of elements such as walks made of aggregate concrete. Pattern is important in walk designs

for adding color, contrast, and interest.

Transparency

Transparency gives depth by overlaps or penetration of vision. Transparency can occur in paving patterns where elements overlap and changes in color make the pattern more interesting.

A sequence of space can be provided by moving from open space to a space with a feeling of enclosure.

Repetition is achieved by the use of bollards with built-in lighting, and rhythm by alternating brick with concrete bands in the paving at Penn Square, Reading, Pennsylvania.

Oldtown Mall,
Baltimore, generally
has a narrow street
width of 45 feet
and, with abutting
buildings of two to
four stories, has an
interesting scale.
(Photograph
courtesy of
O'Malley and
Associates, Inc.)

Space in rectilinear format at Constitution Plaza, Hartford, Connecticut. (Photograph courtesy of Sasaki Associates.)

Transparency is created by overlapping paving elements.

Direction

Direction is a line along which things lie or a reference toward a point or area that gives order to elements. For example, compass direction is often used to orient the system of street layout in a city into north–south and east–west.

Similarity

Similarity occurs when like elements form groups. Repetition, color, shape, size, and texture contribute to this characteristic.

A canopy system used in Wilkes-Barre, Pennsylvania.

Volumes and Enclosure

To achieve clearly defined spaces, we must consider space-forming elements and the volumes contained, such as the base plane, overhead plane, and vertical plane.

BASE PLANES
Base planes relate all objects on a horizontal surface.

VERTICAL PLANES
Vertical planes have an important function in articulating the uses of spaces. Buildings are usually the most important vertical elements in forming spaces. They also act as points of reference or landmarks.

OVERHEAD PLANES
Overhead planes are important in giving definition to the height of a space.

Motion

Motion is a process of moving or changing time or position. It reinforces direction or distance and can give a sense of form in motion. As observers walk along a mall or streetscape, their point of reference or angle of vision of objects changes. This provides a variety of views and sunlight and shadow patterns, depending on the time of day and season of the year.

Time

Continuity over a period of time, or the sequential relationship that any event has to any other, past, present, or future, is important. For example, as new buildings are added to an urban area they can be related to older structures by the use of materials, proportion of architectural elements, texture, and color. Preserving old structures in a city and adding or infilling with new structures provides continuity with our past heritage.

Sensory Quality

The sense of a place—its visual impression, and its appeal to one's senses of sound, smell, and touch—adds a further dimension to the design of urban spaces. Do people relate to or feel at ease in a particular place? Features that please the senses can give a mall or plaza an atmosphere that attracts people. Fountains, sculpture, shaded areas in which to sit and view other people, and appealing activities all help create this environment.

The Sparks Street
Mall in Ottawa,
Ontario, Canada
with its fountains,
overhead planted
canopies, lighting,
and entrance gate-
way. (Photograph
by Ewald Richter.)

5

Design Elements and Street Furniture

Designing and choosing furnishings for a mall, streetscape, or plaza should be approached in the context of both the comprehensive urban environment of the city and the specific location where the furnishings are to be used.

Furnishings are often selected from catalogues without sufficient data on performance. This practice can perpetuate the visual disorder that we wish to eliminate.

The design of a mall or plaza must consider the type, size, scale, location, and materials of all street furnishings.

These elements include paving, lighting, graphic design, sculpture, fountains, bollards, seating, planters, telephones, kiosks, shelters, canopies, trash containers, and drinking fountains.

The design, detailing, and choice of materials of the furnishings are important not only for design continuity but also for both durability and ease of maintenance. Appropriate detailing and use of materials in the urban landscape are therefore of primary importance to the success of a mall, streetscape, or plaza. Experienced urban designers and landscape architects should be involved in the design and coordination of this phase of the project development.

PAVING

Scale, pattern, color, and texture are form characteristics related to the design of the city floor or paving concept for a mall. The paving pattern gives order to the overall design of a mall. It also provides a sense of scale by the use of materials such as brick, concrete, and stone. The slope of the paving and the way in which water runoff is handled are also important items that should be considered.

Fountain, Copley Square, Boston, Massachusetts.

Pavers

Pavers may be set on concrete or bituminous bases or placed on 1 inch of sand above a crushed stone base.

CONCRETE

Concrete pavers are made in many shapes, sizes, and textures. Some newer types are available in a 3-inch thickness, look like brick, and have interlocking shapes for added stability. This material may be placed on sand above a crushed stone base and is strong enough for automobile or bus traffic when used for a semi-mall or transit mall.

Concrete may also be poured in place. A variety of textures are available with this material. Poured concrete may also be used with brick pavers, textured or aggregate concrete pavers, or stone pavers to form paving patterns.

BRICK

Brick, the oldest artificial material, offers a durable, long lasting surface requiring little maintenance. Brick offers a great variety of textures and colors, is available in many sizes and shapes, and provides a hard surface resistant to wear and cracking. Pavers for walks are often 4 × 8 × 1.5 inches and may be arranged in many different patterns.

This clock tower located on Nicollet Mall, Minneapolis, is 21 feet high with a 4-foot square face. The lower portion of the clock has an animated sculpture. (Photograph courtesy of the Downtown Council of Minneapolis.)

STONE

Stone, one of the oldest paving materials, offers a long lasting surface needing little maintenance. Granite is one of the most durable of stones and is often used in urban areas. For added interest it can be used as granite sets, which have a good texture, for paving minor circulation areas such as those used for seating, berms, and areas around trees, fountains, or sculptures.

ASPHALT

Asphalt may be used in the form of pavers or dumped in place. Although asphalt does not have the variety of textures of concrete, it provides a softer walking surface. Asphalt pavers come in a variety of shapes, such as hexagonals, and offer a choice of colors and aggregates.

The color of the material is an important aesthetic factor in the paving design. Color adds interest, particularly in areas with limited amounts of sunshine. Some colors will be compatible with materials used on buildings along the mall or may contrast with these buildings to provide interest. In areas with much sunshine, light-colored materials such as natural concrete tend to reflect light, which is uncomfortable to the pedestrian's vision. This factor must therefore be considered in the choice of materials in the design concept.

Concrete Z-brick interlocking pavers are used on the lower Main Street Mall, Patterson, New Jersey and Wyoming Avenue Plaza, Scranton, Pennsylvania.

Brick pavers laid in running bond are usually set on a concrete slab with ⅜-inch mortar joints or on a bituminous base with tight joints.

Smooth concrete bands with aggregate infill provide an interesting textured effect for walk areas.

Brick and granite paving pattern at Copley Square, Boston.

Brick and concrete are often used to form paving patterns, as at Essex Mall, Salem, Massachusetts.

Granite sets give color and texture to special types of areas such as the cross walks at Essex Mall, Salem, Massachusetts.

Granite paving pattern, Dallas, Texas Arts District Streetscape.

Asphalt pavers are used in similar ways to concrete and are good for walk areas. Because of their dark color, they also reduce glare from reflected sunlight.

Durability and Ease of Maintenance

Durability and ease of maintenance are imporant factors in selecting paving materials. Low cost of initial installation may not be as important in the long run as low maintenance costs. In areas where snow removal is a consideration, materials resistant to salt or other snow melting chemicals should be reviewed. The provision of underground snow melting equipment may also be a consideration in the design of the mall or plaza.

TREE GRATES

Tree grates may become part of the paving pattern of a mall or plaza. When trees are planted directly in the base plane of a mall, the grates become an integral design element in the paving pattern.

Tree grates are used to give a wider expanse to walk areas, to allow air and water to reach the roots of a tree, and to limit maintenance of the open areas around trees in paved areas.

Tree grates also add interest in scale, pattern, color, and texture to the urban environment. Expandable grates should be used to allow for tree growth.

LIGHTING

Night lighting extends the time for participation in activities on the mall or urban space. It provides safety and security and adds interest by accenting plantings, fountains, sculpture, buildings, graphics, and other features in the urban context. Night lighting for malls or plazas is often designed by architects and landscape architects working in conjunction with electrical engineers.

Illumination

For comfort and a feeling of security, one must have adequate light to illuminate details and to make objects brighter than the sky. Unless observers are looking directly at a light source, they see only light reflected by surfaces around them. What they actually see is the brightness of light. If brightness is excessive, it becomes glare. Glare interferes with vision and causes loss of contrast between detail and background.

OUTPUT AND MEASUREMENT
To measure the luminous output of lamps, a unit for the light producing power of a light source was established. It is called a lumen and is defined as the rate at which light falls on a 1-square-foot surface area, all parts of which are 1 foot from a surface with the intensity of one candle.

Illumination on a surface is measured in footcandles. A footcandle is defined as the illumination on 1 square foot over which 1 lumen is evenly distributed. This means that 1 footcandle equals 1 lumen per square foot. The footcandle is the unit used in calculating lighting installations.

LIGHT SOURCES
Several types of light sources are available for night lighting. They are incandescent, fluorescent, and high-intensity discharge lamps such as mercury, metal halide, and high-pressure sodium.

Sometimes special openings for the night lighting of trees are combined into the design of the grates, as at Crocker Plaza, San Francisco.

**Lights with cast
iron poles are an
integral element of
the streetscape at
Newburyport,
Massachusetts.**

INCANDESCENT light has a warm, reddish color. Objects are accentuated when this light is used, and texture is distinguishable. With a typical 100-watt A-19 bulb, lamp life is 750 hours with a 1750-lumen output. Extended service bulbs are available that last 2500 to 8000 hours but have a somewhat lower lumen output.

Another type of incandesent light called a quartz line is often used for spotlights or floodlights. These bulbs have about a 2000-hour lamp life and, at 100 watts, produce 1900 lumens.

Although the initial cost of incandescent fixtures is less by $50 to $75 than that of mercury lamps, the operating cost is higher. Because of its warm color, incandescent light is best on yellow, red, and brown objects and is very desirable in pedestrian areas where warm color is important.

FLUORESCENT lamps produce a dull, flat light with dark objects viewed in silhouette. Fluorescent bulbs come in bluish, yellowish, or pinkish colors. A 100-watt fluorescent bulb has a lamp life of 12,000 to 18,000 hours and produces about 6300 lumens. Cool white lamps produce a neutral to moderately cool effect with good color acceptance.

Fluorescent lamps have increased efficiency over incandescent lamps, but lamp efficiency varies with cold temperature conditions unless a cold weather ballast and enclosed fixture are used. Fluorescent lighting also has a higher initial cost than incandescent.

MERCURY VAPOR has a sparkling quality. It gives two and a half times more light than do incandescent fixtures for the power used. A 100-watt mercury bulb has a lamp life of 24,000 hours with an output of 4200 lumens. Mercury also maintains a high output of lumens over its lamp life. Clear mercury lamps have a cool, greenish color and are good for lighting green objects such as plants.

Deluxe mercury lamps have been improved in color with red, yellow, and blue strengthened. These lamps have good color acceptance and are

Cast iron poles and luminaires at Public Works Museum, Inner Harbor area, Baltimore, Maryland.

Lights with specially designed luminaires are used in the streetscape design in Hollywood, Florida.

These globes are mounted on 14-foot high poles topped by Philadelphia's 1976 bicentennial symbol. (Photograph courtesy of Rohm and Haas Company.)

In the Chestnut Street Transitway, Philadelphia, clusters of eight smoky gray Plexiglas, acrylic plastic globes are used. (Photograph courtesy of Rohm and Haas Company.)

often used to light pedestrian or street areas.

METAL HALIDE is similar to mercury. It is very efficient, giving about an 8000-lumen output at 100 watts with a 10,000-hour life.

HIGH-PRESSURE SODIUM offers small lamp size and good light control. It has a very high efficiency and, for 100 watts, gives about a 9500-lumen output with a 12,000-hour life. It provides a warm, yellowish light and is used for street lighting.

STREET LIGHTING

Although some cities have lighting levels of from 10 to 20 footcandles in core areas, many cities have lower levels. The Illuminating Engineering Society calls for a minimum of 1.2 footcandles on collector streets in commercial areas. At signalized intersections, there should be lighting with at least three times the intensity of street lighting.

In lighting city areas, glare can be a problem if high-intensity lights less

than 35 feet in height are used. If lower lights are used, cut-off shields often help to minimize glare.

MALL AND PLAZA LIGHTING

Light standards in relation to pedestrian scale generally have a maximum height of 12 feet. Where steps are present, care should be taken to provide adequate light to illuminate these areas.

For comfort in viewing lights with clear acrylic globes, it is best to use no

Cast iron pole and luminaire used at Battery Park City in New York.

more than a 75-watt mercury bulb with a refractor over it. There are also fixtures that reflect light downward without the need for seeing the light source. These lights, while giving good illumination, are generally easier on the eyes of the viewer. Several of these fixtures use either 100- or 175-watt mercury bulbs. They also come in a wide range of shapes such as cubes or form circular or rectangular volumes.

GRAPHIC DESIGN

Signs

A comprehensive system of signs is needed for central city areas and for a mall. Signs are part of the overall graphic design for a city. They convey messages that are essential to the function, safety, and security of a mall.

In general, signs conveying the same information in the central city area should be consistent in color, shape, message, and location. They should be easily recognizable in the urban context. Signs must also relate to the varying modes of circulation. Different systems are needed for pedestrians and for motorists. Signs should, for example, prepare a driver in advance for turning decisions or for various road conditions. There are

four basic purposes for which signs are needed: to provide mall identity, to improve traffic flow, to identify commercial facilities, and to provide information on the direction or location of activities.

MALL IDENTITY
A symbol or logo can be very important in giving identity to a mall. The logo can also be useful for public relations purposes.

TRAFFIC SIGNS
Traffic signs include a wide range of signs from highway route markers to parking signs, stop signs, pedestrian crosswalk signs, and direction signs. In developing a mall, it should be determined who has charge of signage for the city or town, and who sets the design standards for these signs. Confusing signs that clutter the downtown environment should be removed as part of an overall program for central city graphics improvement.

Providing information at intersections can be simplified by combining street names and traffic signals on the same pole. This should also be more economical because fewer poles, bases, and wires are needed. Often street lighting, crosswalk directions, and trash containers can also be combined in the same unit.

COMMERCIAL IDENTITY
Signs placed on buildings to identify various shops along a mall should be considered in the overall context of the block. Each sign should be appropriate in size, scale, color, material, and message to the building's architectural character and should be placed conveniently for pedestrian viewing.

Towns and cities should develop ordinances that determine what the maximum size of signs may be, whether they may overhang onto public areas, and which type of illumination is permitted.

INFORMATIONAL SIGNS
Informational signs include directories, maps, and special signs such as those indicating the location of parking areas, subways, and bus systems. These signs give direction to pedestrians and help them locate a particular structure such as a restaurant, department store, or office building.

SIGN MESSAGE
The letter size in a message depends on the distance at which the sign is to be viewed, its location, and its lighting. Letter height should also be appropriate to the sign's setting.

LEGIBILITY
The typeface should be plain in style and form, the proportion and shape

Traffic signal system used on Hamilton Mall, Allentown, Pennsylvania.

**Directory for
Gallery Place,
Washington, D.C.**

**Milles Sculpture at
The Missouri
Botanical Garden,
St. Louis, Missouri.**

familiar, and the weight heavy enough to be effective when seen from a distance.

COLOR

Color is often necessary to differentiate one kind of information from another. For example, red might be used for direction, blue for information, and green for identification.

Graphics may also include banners, flags, wind socks, and other displays that add interest and color to the urban scene.

SCULPTURE

Sculpture and other works of art such as fountains and wall reliefs are important elements in improving the quality of the urban environment. These elements enhance the sensory quality of a place and help create an atmosphere where people wish to be.

Architects should meet with a sculptor in the early stages of a project to discuss the setting for a sculpture and to consult on its scale, form, mass, and color. Outdoor sculpture must have adequate mass to stand out against its background. Mass is the feeling of weight and volume that a sculpture imparts to an observer.

Size, Scale, and Form

The size and scale of a sculpture should be appropriate to its setting, which in an urban area comprises the buildings and space of which it will become an integral part. A sculpture must be large enough to have an impact on its surroundings. The form of a sculpture, that is, its shape and structure, will either blend or contrast with its setting. There is an infinite variety of forms that can be created in sculpture. These forms are expressed in particular materials.

Materials and Color

Materials for outdoor sculpture should be durable and resistant to urban pollution. Stone, metal, masonry, and in some cases newer materials, such as plastics, are used. Color is related to the type of material, such as granite, bronze, or

Weathering Steel Sculpture by Louise Nevelson, Government Center, Binghamton, New York.

Bronze sculpture by Barbara Hepworth, Balboa Park, San Diego.

Sculpture made of stone on granite base called Passage by Manuel Neri at Christina Gateway, Wilmington, Delaware.

stainless steel. Metals can easily be painted, and a wide range of colors is available. Plastics also offer a wide choice of colors.

A sculpture is often viewed from several directions, and the foreground as well as the background should be considered in placing the sculpture.

Orientation is also very important in relation to how and where a sculpture is placed. Sunlight and shadow patterns vary at different times of the day and with seasonal changes. There should also be enough room around the sculpture for maximum viewing from varying sight lines and for walking around it, or perhaps for viewing while sitting.

The way in which a sculpture meets the ground or sits on a base is important in terms of both its height and the way in which it is viewed. A sculpture may begin at grade or may be elevated on a base, placed in a planter, designed as part of a fountain, or anchored to or from a building.

Weight and installation are other important considerations in placing a sculpture. A special foundation may be needed, or equipment such as a crane may be required to set the sculpture in place.

Night Lighting

Night lighting effects on the sculpture give added interest. The location and angle of the lights, the amount of light, and the type of fixture are all important. Light may be directed from above or below, from the background or foreground, or from a combination of these.

Landfall by Ned Smyth at Christina Gateway, Wilmington, Delaware represents the Swedes landing at what is now Wilmington.

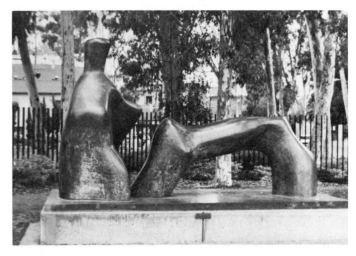

Bronze sculpture in Balboa Park, San Diego.

Polished bronze sculpture on stone base by Arnaldo Pomodoro, Hirshorn National Sculpture Garden, Washington, D.C.

Bronze sculpture on raised base in Portland, Oregon.

FOUNTAINS

Fountains and pools are often the focal elements of a mall or plaza. Water, a natural element, has many unique qualities when used in fountains. The sound of water, its cooling effect, and its reflective qualities provide the designer with a wide range of creative possibilities.

Sculptural Elements

Fountains often have sculptural elements as part of their design. The sculpture acts as the focus during all seasons of the year, particularly in climatic areas where water cannot be used during the winter. The orientation of the fountain determines how the reflection of sunlight off the water or on the sculptural elements will add interest.

Water Effects

The effects of water must be carefully worked out. Many different uses of sprays, jets, waterfalls, and reflecting pools are possible. Nozzles are available in a variety of sizes and effects. By means of swivels a nozzle may be rotated about 15 degrees in all directions. This affords flexibility in aiming the water in a particular direction. An individual nozzle can use as little as 1 to 2 gallons of water per minute, depending on the desired effect. Many small fountains with the combined effects of the nozzles use several hundred gallons of water per minute, with larger ones recirculating thousands of gallons per minute. The Civic Center Forecourt Fountain in Portland uses over 13,000 gallons per minute in its waterfall effect (see p. 214).

Fountain Details

Many factors are involved in the design of fountains.

Sculpture in fountain called Sunrise by Xavier Corbero, Christina Gateway, Wilmington, Delaware.

Bronze sculpture
and fountain at
Williams Square,
Las Colinas, Irving,
Texas.

Fountain at Harvard
University,
Cambridge,
Massachusetts.

BOTTOMS

The bottoms of fountains are often painted black to add reflective qualities to the surface of a pool and to give the impression of depth. Pool bottoms may be paved with stone, brick, or tile.

EDGES, COPINGS, OR STEPS

These elements depend on the function of the fountain. Some fountains are designed for people to wade in or walk through, while other fountains are for viewing only.

COPINGS are generally used to act as safety barriers, to define the edge of a fountain, to provide a place for sitting, and to overhang fountain equipment and thus limit the view of nozzles and water overflow controls.

MATERIALS

The choice of appropriate materials for fountains is an integral part of their design. These materials must be weather and crack resistant. Poured-in-place concrete is often used to form a pool and coping. Stone, brick, or tile can be placed over concrete as a base. The materials should also be stain resistant. If weathering steel is used for a sculpture, the material and color of the fountain bottom should be chosen so as to limit problems from the stains. Precast concrete is often used for fountain elements such as bowls from which water pours. This material is durable and crack resistant. It can also be used for copings or for pool bottoms on top of a concrete base.

Waterproofing membranes should be used to prevent water from causing problems beneath a fountain in areas with frost or on rooftops of buildings where leaks can be a critical problem. Membranes can be sprayed on or applied from rolls, as is roofing material, and installed in a similar manner.

MECHANICAL SYSTEMS

Mechanical systems for fountains should be designed by mechanical engineers experienced in fountain design. Mechanical systems are usually designed to allow for more capacity in gallons per minute than the minimum necessary for fountain operation so that, if a larger volume of water is desired than was originally estimated, it will be available. Pipe size should therefore be one size larger than the minimum, as should the pump, which can then be throttled down so that it does not have to run at maximum efficiency to give the desired effects. If a storage tank for recirculating water is part of the fountain equipment, it should also have reserve capacity.

PIPING

Piping for fountains is generally copper with brass nozzles. If galvanized pipe is used and is connected to copper, electrolysis will result in chemical decomposition where the materials are joined. Dielectric fittings are made to limit this problem.

Drains are placed in the pool bottom for cleaning or for draining the pool to winterize it. There are also filtering systems, chlorine injectors if people are to wade in the pools, wind controls, and automatic controls to compensate for water evaporation or

Fountain and reflecting pool at Christian Science Church, Boston, Massachusetts.

Fountain at Civic Center, Albuquerque, New Mexico.

Waterfall effect at Morton D. May Memorial Amphitheatre in downtown St. Louis, Missouri.

Bronze Dolphin Sculpture as a feature in the fountain at the Aquarium, Boston, Massachusetts.

Equidon Plaza, Del Mar, California: A change of 30 feet in elevation was used to create a cascading effect in this courtyard as water flows over the granite slabs that step down the site.

Fountain at Water Gardens, Fort Worth, Texas.

Fountain with waterfall at Fountain Place, Allied Bank Tower, Dallas, Texas.

77

spillage. A completely automatic system can be used to turn the fountain on and off at specified times and to control the equipment in the fountain.

A room close to or beneath the fountain will be necessary for the mechanical equipment. There must be adequate space to service this equipment easily.

Night Lighting

Night lighting gives an added effect to fountains. Lighting can be very dramatic, and sequences of different water and lighting effects can be pro-grammed. When lights are flush with the bottom of pools, they must be winterized in cold climates. Special attention must be given to this, or the light housings may crack over the winter. Protective covers are made for some types of lights to keep them dry when the fountain is drained. The lights must also be drained and, if not covered, must be sealed with a special gasket. Lights set flush in the bottom of pools are water cooled and need at least a 2- to 3-inch depth of water above them. Lights set above pool bottoms usually require a 14-inch depth to allow for the light and for a cooling effect.

View of fountain with waterfall at Fountain Place, Allied Bank Tower, Dallas, Texas.

View of fountain sequence at Fountain Place, Allied Bank Tower, Dallas, Texas.

Sequence of water with computerized fountain at Fountain Place, Allied Bank Tower, Dallas, Texas.

The fountain at Commerce Square, Philadelphia has a granite coping and bottom. A granite seating wall defines the space around the fountain.

Recreational pool and fountain area at St. Louis Station.

Fountain at Mellon
Square, Pittsburgh,
Pennsylvania.

BOLLARDS

Bollards should be considered as an integral design element when used on a mall or plaza. They act as a barrier separating traffic from pedestrian areas. They also increase interest by setting up rhythm and providing scale, texture, and color. Bollards are often combined with chains to reinforce the feeling of separation or to help form a barrier. The use of chains also allows bollards to be spaced at a wider interval when this is necessary. Bollards often are combined with night lighting to illuminate pedestrian areas or the roadway of a semimall or transit mall.

SEATING

The type and the placement of sitting areas are important to how a mall functions. Generally, sitting areas are set back from the major circulation lines on a mall. Sitting areas should also have protection from the sun, as people prefer to sit in shaded areas.

Benches

Benches are made of wood, metal, concrete, or stone. They are usually 15 or 16 inches above grade for seating comfort and often are designed with backs. Wooden benches are the most comfortable but must be built of durable materials to limit vandalism.

Concrete or stone benches, especially ones without backs, may be used in some areas of a mall or plaza and may act as sculptural elements. Benches are often combined with raised planters or walls, and in full malls are sometimes placed toward the center of the pedestrian street and separated from major circulation by the planters or walls. In hot climates or areas directly exposed to the sun, benches are designed as parts of structures containing lattice work to provide shade.

The tops of walls or planters may also serve as sitting areas if designed at an appropriate height. This procedure can greatly expand the amount of seating on a mall or plaza.

Bollards are used in this streetscape at The Municipal Pier, St. Petersburg, Florida.

Granite bollards were designed for this streetscape at Newburyport, Massachusetts.

Bench on plaza, Newburyport, Massachusetts.

Wood and cast iron benches, Copley Square, Boston, Massachusetts.

TREE PLANTERS AND POTS

Many types of planters are available for both trees and flowers. Pots for trees must have at least a 3-foot depth and be well drained. These pots can be designed in a variety of materials such as wood, concrete and stone, or asbestos concrete. Flower pots can be placed in a variety of locations to add interest and color to urban areas. Pots are also versatile and may be moved and rearranged for special or seasonal displays.

Concrete and wood bench, Penn Square, Reading.

Low street tree planter with built in seating at River City Mall, Louisville, Kentucky. (Photograph courtesy Lynne Rubenstein.)

Polished granite seating area at the World Financial Center Plaza, Battery Park City, New York.

TELEPHONES

Public telephones have been placed in a variety of enclosures or booths. Many new units are designed without booths; these provide ease of maintenance and less opportunity for vandalism. Partial weather and sound control has been studied for these newer models, and coin collection is practically vandalproof in many units.

KIOSKS, SHELTERS, AND CANOPIES

Kiosks, shelters, and canopies are often needed in central city areas.

Kiosks

Kiosks are well suited for pedestrian malls and have been used for bulletin boards, street directories, display cases, and information booths. They act as focal elements and also add color, help set or maintain a particular mood, and often provide night lighting.

Shelters

Shelters may be used on malls to provide sitting areas protected from the climatic factors of sunlight, wind, and

Flower pots, Main Street Mall, Charlottesville, Virginia.

Flower pots used in streetscape on original Nicollet Mall in Minneapolis.

Telephone booths at Faneuil Hall Marketplace, Boston, Massachusetts.

precipitation. These shelters become architectural features of the mall.

BUS SHELTERS

Bus shelters to provide weather protection for transit users may also be required, depending on the prevailing length of waiting time and the amount of protection from the elements offered on the street.

Some of these shelters incorporate newsstands and telephone booths and may be heated in areas with severe climates.

Canopies

Canopies have been used in the design of several malls. They provide weather protection and often act as a unifying architectural element. Appropriate choice of materials, structural system, and form can help to create a certain mood or sense of place for the mall. Lighting can be incorporated into the design of the canopies and can give additional continuity to the design.

Canopies have been built with a variety of structural systems. Some

Kiosk, Main Street Mall, Charlottesville, Virginia.

Kiosk, Essex Mall, Salem, Massachusetts.

have been made of steel or aluminum, some of wood, and others of concrete.

For weather protection the top of the canopy is often made of aluminum with plexiglas infill, but in some cases other materials have been used.

CLOCKS, TRASH CONTAINERS, AND DRINKING FOUNTAINS

Other items of street furniture include clocks, trash containers, and drinking fountains, all of which are part of the urban context.

Clocks

Clocks act as focal elements and add to the interest of a mall or plaza while also serving a useful function. A clock may also be a focus of a space and can act as a landmark.

Trash Containers

Trash receptacles are available in a wide variety of shapes and sizes. Many are built of wood with plastic liners; others are made of concrete, metal, or plastic.

Drinking Fountains

Drinking fountains are a functional element in pedestrian areas. They are made of many materials, such as pre-cast concrete, metal, stone, or masonry. Fountains are also available in models that accommodate a wheel-chair. Drinking fountains may also act as sculptural elements and add interest to a mall or plaza. Freeze-proof types are available to limit problems in climates with frost.

Shelter, Ithaca Commons. (Photograph courtesy of Anton J. Egner and Associates.)

Kiosk shelter at Levi Plaza, San Francisco.

Shelter at River City Mall, Louisville, Kentucky. (Photograph courtesy of Lynne Rubenstein.)

Transparent roofed bus shelters have been installed on the Chestnut Street Transitway, Philadelphia. (Photograph courtesy of Rohm and Haas Company.)

Canopy at Hamilton Mall, Allentown, Pennsylvania.

Canopy in downtown Wilkes-Barre, Pennsylvania is a distinctive part of the streetscape design.

Canopy, Market Square Mall, Knoxville, Tennessee. (Photograph courtesy of Downtown Knoxville Association, Inc.)

Clock tower on granite pedestal at Lincoln Plaza, Dallas, Texas.

Sculptural clock tower at the Fulton Mall, Fresno, California.

Clock, Federal Building, Wilmington, Delaware.

**Concrete trash
container.**

**Metal trash
container.**

**Drinking fountain
in Lansing,
Michigan. (Photo-
graph courtesy of
Johnson, Johnson
and Roy, Inc.)**

Precast concrete drinking fountain.

Concrete drinking fountain for the disabled.

(preceding pages)

The use of plant material is an integral part of the design concept of a mall or urban space. (Photograph courtesy of Anton J. Egner and Associates.)

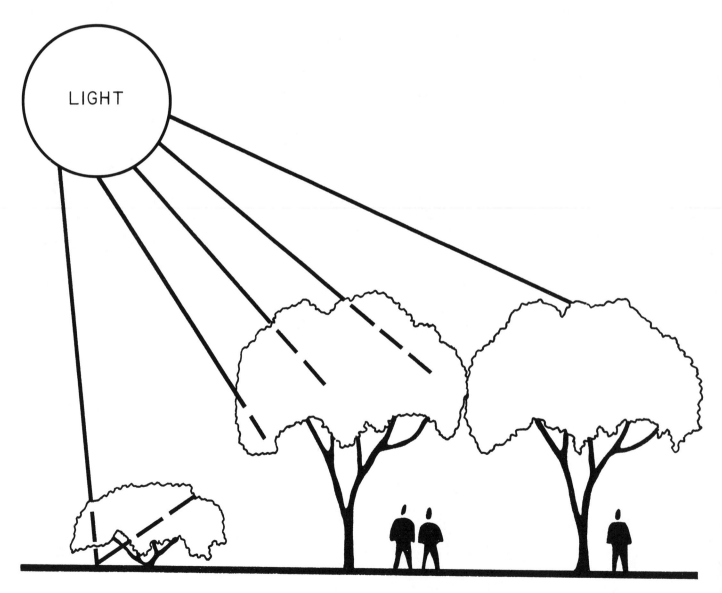

Plants control solar radiation.

6

Plants in the City

In the past, many professionals in planning, architecture, and engineering considered the use of plants in urban areas mostly in terms of aesthetics. Recently, however, research has established the value of plants for climatic control, environmental engineering, and architectural uses. These uses have functional and economic benefit also.

CLIMATIC USES

Microclimate

Microclimate refers to local variations in climate, as distinguished from the climate of an overall region. Climatic factors that affect pedestrians are solar radiation, temperature, air movement, humidity, and precipitation.

SOLAR RADIATION
Solar radiation provides light and heat. Much of this radiation is reflected away from the planet by clouds; part is diffused by particles in our atmosphere; some is absorbed by oxides, water vapor, and ozone; and the remainder, about 20 percent, reaches the earth's surface. Some of the solar radiation, referred to as short-wave radiation, penetrates the earth's surface and is absorbed by the ground, buildings, paving, plants, and other objects. Solar radiation heats these objects, which then reradiate heat in the form of long-wave radiation.

Control of solar radiation depends on interception or reflection. Trees offer one of the best controls for solar radiation; they may block sunlight or filter it. Temperatures are much cooler beneath shade trees, and in effect trees provide a natural air conditioning system. This system operates with solar radiation, absorbing carbon dioxide, heat, and water and transpiring cool air in the form of water vapor. Mature trees may transpire as much as 100 gallons of water per day. This provides the cooling effect of five 10,000-British thermal unit air conditioners working 20 hours per day.

There is also a greater sense of comfort in shaded areas because of reduced long-wave radiation and lack of glare.

Scientists at the University of Indiana found that, with an air temperature of 84°F, the surface temperature of a concrete street was 108°F. Where the street was lined with trees, surface temperatures dropped 20°F.

WIND
Wind helps to control temperatures. If wind is of low velocity, it may be pleasant. As its velocity increases, however, it may cause discomfort or damage. Plants control wind by forming barriers or obstructions, and by providing guidance, deflection, and filtration. Trees as barriers reduce windspeed by their resistance to windflow.

Urban winds are produced by convection and by constriction. Convection currents are created when air is heated by buildings, streets, and automobiles and then rises. Larger, taller buildings add greater heat to the air, causing it to rise faster and to draw air from the street toward the buildings. Convection currents usually are no problem for pedestrians.

The second effect is created by constriction of air as it travels down streets separating the linear facades of urban structures. This wind is attributed to the Venturi principle: air speeds up as a space becomes constricted. In cities the Venturi effect is determined by building height, street length, and street width.

Wind from the combined factors of convection and the Venturi effect can cause gusts felt by pedestrians. Street trees can buffer these winds at pedestrian level and filter out much of the dust and debris they stir up.

PRECIPITATION
Plants help to control the amount of precipitation reaching the ground. By intercepting precipitation and slowing it down, plants aid in moisture retention and the prevention of soils ero-

sion. They also help the soil retain its moisture by providing shade and protection from wind.

ENVIRONMENTAL ENGINEERING

Air Purification

Plants clean the air through the process of photosynthesis and the emission of oxygen. One hundred fifty square meters of leaf surface is needed to meet the yearly oxygen requirements of each person. The minimum ratio of parts of contaminated usable air for people is 1:3000.

Air pollution is caused by hydrocarbons, carbon oxides, sulfur oxides, photochemical oxides, thermal matter, and particulate matter.

Trees use carbon dioxide for photosynthesis. Auto exhausts account for much of the carbon dioxide in urban areas. Sulfur dioxide, also a product of fuel combustion, is prevalent in the burning of coal and in the exhausts of heating oils and automobiles. Experiments indicate that trees aid in eliminating sulfur dioxide from the air by absorption into leaves and by entrapment on their surfaces. Ozone, a photochemical oxidant, is produced by lightning and by sunlight activating auto exhaust materials. Ozone combines readily with other substances and acts as a reagent with sulfur dioxide and ozone before they combine to form sulfuric acid. Plants aid in eliminating this dangerous pollutant. Trees also help filter out up to 75 percent of particulate air pollutants such as dust, pollen, smoke, odors, and fumes, thus making the air more healthful for pedestrians.

Noise

Unwanted sound is referred to as noise. Noise is a problem especially in urban areas.

Sound waves are measured in cycles per second, with the range of human hearing from 20 to 20,000 cycles per second. The level of sound is measured in decibels. The sound level of a normal conversation is about 60 decibels, whereas a plane taking off may produce 120 decibels at a 200-foot distance. Sound energy

from a source usually spreads out and dissipates in transmission. Sound waves can be absorbed, reflected, deflected, or refracted. Trees absorb sound waves through their leaves, branches, and twigs. Plants with thick, fleshy leaves and thin petioles, such as the littleleaf linden, are best for this purpose. The trunks and branches of trees deflect sound, reducing the sound level. Also, wind moving through trees creates sounds that are pleasant and mask unwanted noise. It has been estimated that a 100-foot depth of forest reduces sound between the source and the observer by about 21 decibels.

Glare

Trees and shrubs reduce glare and reflection. Glare can be caused by sunlight, especially in the early morning and late afternoon, or by an artificial source such as street lights or automobile headlights. A bright light source received directly is called primary glare. Light from a primary source such as the sun causes some glare, no matter what its angle in the sky.

Reflection

Reflection of light is called secondary glare. Natural reflective surfaces are water, sand, and rock; man-made reflectors are materials such as glass, metal, chrome, brick, concrete, and painted surfaces. Atmospheric particles, which cause light to scatter, also produce secondary glare.

Plants may be used to block or filter primary glare. When the sources of glare and reflection are identified, plants having the correct size, shape, and foliage density may be placed so as to solve the problem.

Erosion Control

Plants may also be used on slopes or flat areas to prevent erosion from water runoff. Plants may be not only effective for this use but also economical as compared to the cost of paving sloped areas. Erosion is also minimized when leaves or branches intercept rain and minimize splashing, when roots hold soil, and when organic matter from plants increases soil absorption.

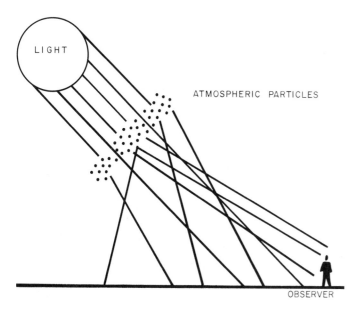

Illustration of glare.

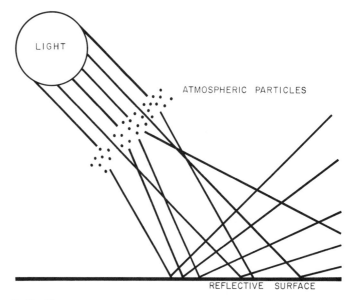

Reflection.

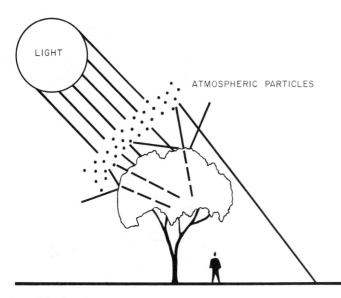

Trees block primary glare.

ARCHITECTURAL AND AESTHETIC USES

In using trees for architectural and aesthetic effects, one must consider that it takes an average of 35 years for most trees to reach maturity. The estimated average life of many buildings under construction today is 50 years. Therefore, when small trees are planted, many years pass before the trees provide an effective canopy for shade as well as other environmental and architectural benefits. For use in cities, trees with trunks 5 to 6 inches in caliper or larger are in proper scale with buildings and other elements. They also help to relate tall buildings to human scale.

Space Definition

Plants can be used as walling elements, as canopies, or as part of the base plane. As walling elements, plants can create outdoor spaces. Bosques of trees form a large canopy of shade under which sitting areas may be developed.

Screening

Trees and shrubs can screen out objectionable views. Evergreen plants are most effective for this purpose.

Continuity

Trees can provide a sense of continuity by their use in urban areas. Trees are used to line many streets in European cities, such as Paris, and to provide canopies of shaded areas in which pedestrians can walk.

Trees as Sculpture

Trees can act as sculptural elements forming the focal points of a space. Trees are interesting for their form, branch structure, texture, and color.

View Control

Trees may complement a design or provide the setting or backdrop for outdoor sculpture. They may also provide filtered views of buildings or spaces. This filtering gives added interest and softens the urban environment of buildings and paving.

Trees also may serve to frame a view and thus maximize its dramatic effect. In addition, plants accent architecture; for example, they reinforce entry to a building or space, or they articulate space, setting up a sequence of spaces where desirable.

Tree growth in 10 years. (Reproduced from "How Fast Do Trees Grow?" by E. L. Kemmerer, Morton Arboretum Bulletin of Popular Information.)

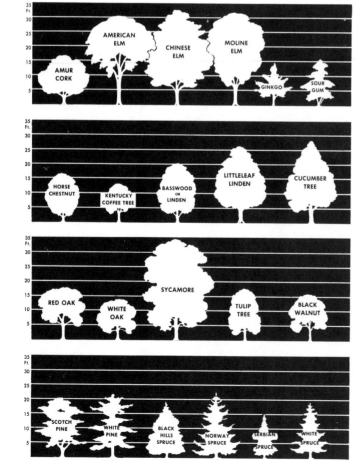

Trees form a shaded promenade area at The Esplanade, Battery Park City, New York.

Trees provide canopies over pedestrian walks.

Filtered view of Paley Plaza, New York, with waterfall in background.

Henry Moore, Reclining Figure with a backdrop of terraced areas and Ginkgo trees at the Sculpture Garden, Nelson-Atkins Museum of Art in Kansas City, Missouri. The garden was designed by Dan Kiley.

Mood

Plants also affect people's moods, providing privacy and a sense of springtime as new leaves unfold and flowers bloom.

CRITERIA FOR SELECTION OF PLANT MATERIAL

In selecting plant material for use in urban areas, a site assessment of existing conditions should be made. For example, is there adequate space for root growth? Where are utility lines located? Is there standing water on-site? What are the characteristics of the microclimate? These and other questions must be reviewed and analyzed before plant material is selected. One must be concerned with hardiness, form and structure, color, and foliage, flowers, and fruit, as well as with safety and maintenance.

Hardiness

A specific tree, shrub, or ground cover must be hardy in the region of the country where it is to be planted. Hardiness depends primarily on temperature, but precipitation and soil properties, such as degree of acidity or alkalinity, called pH, are also important items to consider. For example, sweet gums do not like temperatures below zero, and hemlocks prefer an acidic soil.

In what type of soil condition will the tree, shrub, or ground cover grow? For example, red maples will grow in wet soil but also adapt to other soils; horse chestnuts need moisture, and their leaves will turn brown if the soil is too dry; dogwoods need well-drained soil and cannot tolerate wet areas. Will the trees survive in city conditions? Lindens are very tolerant of air pollution, as are honey locusts and London plane trees. (See Table 6-1, pages 104 to 106.)

Trees help articulate space at Central City Mall, Williamsport, Pennsylvania.

Hardiness zones of the United States and Canada. (Compiled by the Arnold Arboretum, Harvard University, Jamaica Plain, Massachusetts, May 1, 1967.)

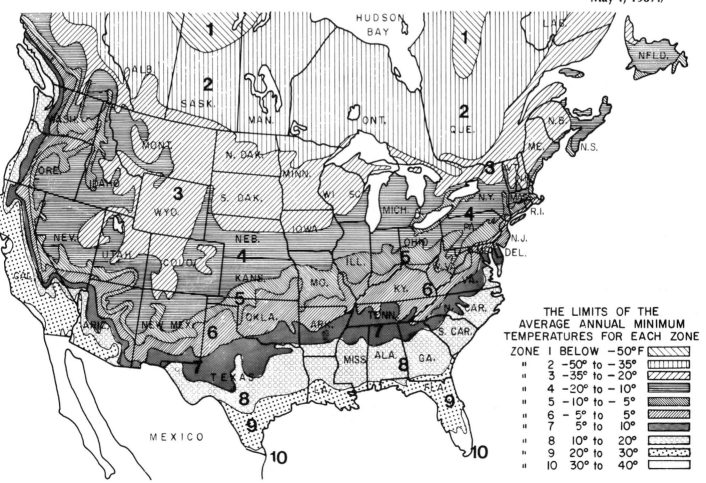

THE LIMITS OF THE
AVERAGE ANNUAL MINIMUM
TEMPERATURES FOR EACH ZONE

ZONE	1	BELOW	$-50°$F
"	2	$-50°$ to	$-35°$
"	3	$-35°$ to	$-20°$
"	4	$-20°$ to	$-10°$
"	5	$-10°$ to	$-5°$
"	6	$-5°$ to	$5°$
"	7	$5°$ to	$10°$
"	8	$10°$ to	$20°$
"	9	$20°$ to	$30°$
"	10	$30°$ to	$40°$

TABLE 6-1　Trees for City Use

LATIN NAME	COMMON NAME	HARDINESS ZONE	FALL (FEET)	HABIT[a]	COLORS	CHARACTERISTICS
		DECIDUOUS TREES				
Acer buergerianum	Trident Maple	6	25	R	Yellow-orange	Dark green foliage Drought tolerant
Acer campestre	Hedge Maple	5–6	35	R	Yellow	Wide range soils Disease resistant
Acer ginnala	Amur Maple	2	18	R	Scarlet	Dark glossy green foliage Easily transplanted
Acer platanoides var.	Norway Maple	3	60	O	Yellow	Dense foliage Wide soil range
Acer platanoides Cleveland	Cleveland	3	60	U	Yellow	Dark green foliage
Acer platanoides Columnare	Columnare	3	60	U	Yellow	Branches 60 to 90° from central trunk
Acer platanoides Crimson King	Crimson King	3	60	O		Purple foliage
Acer platanoides Emerald Queen	Emerald Queen	3	60	O	Yellow	Rapid growth
Acer platanoides Globosum	Globe Norway Maple	3	18	R	Yellow	Small, dense
Acer platanoides summershade	Summershade	3	65	O		Dark green foliage
Acer platanoides pseudoplatanus	Sycamore Maple	5	80	WS		Winged fruit
Acer tataricum	Tatarian Maple	4	20	R	Yellow-red	Rapid growth Drought tolerant
Amelanchier canadensis var.	Shadblow Serviceberry	4	30	U	Yellow-red	Early white flowers, multistem
Amelanchier c. Cumulus	Cumulus Shadblow	4	30	U	Orange-scarlet	Fleecy white flowers
Amelanchier c. Robin Hill Pink	Pink Shadblow	4	30	U	Yellow-red	Pink flowers
Carpinus betulus var.	European Hornbeam	5	40	P	Yellow	Dense foliage
Carpinus betulus Fastigiata		5	40	U	Yellow	Good for screen
Celtis laevigata	Sugar Hackberry	5	70	R		Resistant to witches' broom
Celtis occidentalis Prairie Pride	Prairie Pride	2	60	P	Yellow	Tolerates wide range of soil conditions
Cercidiphyllum japonicum	Katsura-tree	4	60	R	Yellow-apricot	Disease resistant
Corylus colurna	Turkish Filbert	4	70	P	Yellow-purple	Tolerates drought and heat
Crataegus phaenopyrum	Washington Hawthorn	4	25	R	Scarlet-orange	White flowers and orange berries
Crataegus virdis Winter King	Winter King	4	25	R	Scarlet-purple	White flowers and red berries
Eucomia ulmoides	Hardy Rubber Tree	4	60	WS		Disease resistant Lustrous dark green foliage, inter. bark
Fraxinus pennsylvanica lanceolata var.	Green Ash	2	60	R	Yellow	Rapid growth
Fraxinus p. lanceolata Marshall's Seedless Ash	Marshall's Seedless Ash	2	55	R	Yellow	Dark green foliage less insect problems
Fraxinus p. Newport	Newport Green Ash	2	55	U	Yellow	Glossy green foliage
Ginkgo biloba var.	Ginkgo	4	75	R	Yellow	Disease resistant
Ginkgo biloba Autumn Gold	Autumn Gold	4	45	U	Yellow	Male
Ginkgo biloba Fairmount	Fairmount	4	75	P	Yellow	Male
Ginkgo biloba Lakeview	Lakeview	4	50	U	Yellow	Male
Ginkgo biloba Princeton Sentry	Princeton Sentry	4	70	U	Yellow	Male
Gleditsia triancanthos inermis var.	Thornless Honey Locust	4	70	WS	Yellow	
Gleditsia t. inermis Halka	Halka	4	50	R	Yellow	Straight trunk
Gleditsia t. inermis Imperial	Imperial	4	35	WS	Yellow	Dense foliage
Gleditsia t. inermis Majestic	Majestic	4	65	V	Yellow	Dark green foliage
Gleditsia t. inermis Moraine	Moraine	4	80	V	Yellow	
Gleditsia t. inermis Shademaster	Shademaster	4	40	R	Yellow	Disease resistant
Gleditsia t. inermis Skyline	Skyline	4	45	P	Yellow	Leathery foliage
Gleditsia t. inermis Sunburst	Sunburst	4	35	WS	Yellow	Yellow foliage on branch tip
Koelreuteria paniculata	Goldenrain Tree	4	30	R		Yellow flower
Liquidambar styraciflua var.	Sweet Gum	5	60	P	Scarlet	Disease resistant

TABLE 6-1 (*Continued*)

LATIN NAME	COMMON NAME	HARDINESS ZONE	FALL (FEET)	HABIT[a]	COLORS	CHARACTERISTICS
		DECIDUOUS TREES (*Continued*)				
Liquidambar styraciflua Burgundy	Burgundy	5	60	P	Purple	
Liquidambar styraciflua Festival	Festival	5	60	U	Red-yellow	
Liquidambar styraciflua Moraine	Moraine	5	60	O	Scarlet	Fast growth
Metasequoia glyptostroboides	Dawn Redwood	4	100	P	Orange-brown	Good ornamental Likes moist sites
Magnolia soulangeana	Saucer Magnolia	5	20	R	Bronze	Shrublike, white flowers
Magnolia stellata	Star Magnolia	5	20	R	Orange	Shrublike, white flowers
Malus var.	Crabapple					
Malus Adams	Adams	4	20	R		Very disease resistant Red flowers, red fruit
Malus American Beauty	American Beauty	4	20	U		Red flowers Red fruit
Malus baccata	Siberian Crab	2	25	U		White flowers, red-yellow fruit
Malus Baskatong	Baskatong	4	25	U		Red-purple flowers Dark red fruit Very disease resistant
Malus Centurion	Centurion	4	20	U		High disease resistance, rose red flowers, red fruit
Malus Dolgo	Dolgo	3	40	WS		White flowers, red fruit
Malus Donald Wyman	Donald Wyman	4	20	WS		White flowers, red fruit
Malus floribunda	Japanese Flowering Crab	4	25	P	Yellow-orange	Pink-white flowers, red-yellow fruit
Malus Harvest Gold	Harvest Gold	4	20	U		White flowers, gold fruit
Malus Henry Kohankie	Henry Kohankie	4	20	R		White flowers, red fruit
Malus hupensis	Tea Crab	4	20	V		Pink flowers, yellow-red fruit
Malus Katherine	Katherine	4	20	R		Pink flowers, yellow fruit
Malus Liset	Liset	4	15	U		Pink-red flowers, red fruit
Malus Professor Sprenger	Professor Sprenger	4	20	U		Pink bud, white flowers, red fruit
Malus Robinson	Robinson	4	25	U		Deep pink flowers, red fruit
Malus sargenti	Sargent Crab	5	8	R		White flowers, dark red fruit
Malus Sentinel	Sentinel	4	20	U		Pink-white flowers, red fruit
Malus Snowdrift	Snowdrift Crab	3	20	R		White flowers, orange-red fruit
Malus White Angel	White Angel	4	20	U		White flowers, red fruit
Malus zumi calocarpa	Zumi Crab	4	15	P		White flowers, red fruit
Ostrya virginiana	American Hophornbeam	3	40	R	Yellow	Disease resistant
Phellodendron amurense	Amur Cork Tree	3	45	WS	Yellow	Interesting corky bark
Platanus acerifolia var.	London Plane Tree	5	80	WS		Peeling bark
Platanus acerifolia Bloodgood	Bloodgood	5	50	WS		Disease resistant
Prunus sargenti Columnaris	Columnaris Sargent Cherry	4	70	U	Red	Deep pink flowers
Pyrus calleryana var.	Callery Pear	5	30	P	Red	White flowers
Pyrus calleryana Aristocrat	Aristocrat	5	40	O	Crimson	Large foliage
Pyrus calleryana Autumn	Autumn Blaze	5	40	R	Red-purple	White flowers Cold hardy
Pyrus calleryana Chanticleer	Chanticleer	5	40	P	Yellow	Rapid growth
Pyrus calleryana Fauriei	Fauriei	5	15	R	Yellow	Dwarf selection
Pyrus calleryana Redspire	Redspire	5	40	P	Yellow	Shiny dark green leaves
Quercus borealis	Red Oak	4	75	R	Red	Rapid growth
Quercus laurifolia	Laurel Oak	7	60	R		Dense foliage
Quercus palustris var. sovereign	Sovereign Pin Oak	4	75	P	Red	Branching horizontally or ascending
Quercus phellos	Willow Oak	5	50	R	Yellow	Willowlike foliage
Quercus robur Fastigiata	Pyramidal English Oak	4	60	U		Adaptable to soil pH Upright form
Quercus shumardii	Shumard Oak	6	80	R		Tolerant of higher soil pH
Sabal palmetto	Cabbage Palmetto	8	90	Palm		
Salix babylonica	Babylon Weeping Willow	5	40	W	Yellow	Pendulous tolerant of wet or moist sites
Sophora japonica	Japanese Pagoda Tree	4	70	R	Yellow	

TABLE 6-1 (*Continued*)

LATIN NAME	COMMON NAME	HARDINESS ZONE	FALL (FEET)	HABIT[a]	COLORS	CHARACTERISTICS
		DECIDUOUS TREES (*Continued*)				
Sophora japonica Regent	Regent Scholar-tree (Pagodatree)	4	70	R		White flowers in summer
Taxodium distichum	Baldcypress	4	70	U	Russett-brown	Tolerant of wet soil
Tilia cordata var.	Little-leaf Linden	3	60	P	Yellow	Disease resistant Leathery foliage
Tilia cordata Greenspire	Greenspire Linden	3	60	P	Yellow	Disease resistant Leathery foliage
Tilia cordata Chancellor	Chancellor Linden	3	60	P	Yellow	Dense foliage
Tilia cordata Rancho	Rancho Linden	3	60	U	Yellow	Small glossy green leaves
Tilia euchlora	Crimean Linden	3	50	R	Yellow-green	Lustrous dark green foliage
Tilia europaea	European Linden	3	60	R	Yellow	
Tilia tomentosa	Silver Linden	4	80	P		Dark green leaves upper surface
Ulmus americana var. Augustine	Augustine Ascending Elm	2	90	V		Susceptible to Dutch elm disease and necrosis
Ulmus carpinifolia Christine Buisman	Christine Buisman Elm	4	60	V		
Ulmus parviflora	Chinese Elm	4	50	R	Yellow-purple	Good bark, disease resistant
Zelkova serrata var.	Japanese Zelkova	5	60	V	Yellow-russet	
Zelkova Parkview	Parkview	5	60	V	Russet	Disease resistant, consistent form
Zelkova Village Green	Village Green	5	60	V	Russet	Disease resistant, rapid growth
		EVERGREEN TREES				
Abies concolor	White Fir	4	100	P		Blue-green foliage
Cinnamomum camphora	Camphor	9	40	R		Dense, glossy foliage
Magnolia grandiflora	Southern Magnolia	7	100	P		White flowers
Picea pungens	Colorado Spruce	2	80	P		Stiff green to blue foliage
Quercus virginiana	Live Oak	7	60	WS		Fine textured foliage
Taxus cuspidata	Japanese Yew	4	30	P		Red berries
Tsuga caroliniana	Carolina Hemlock	4	75	P		Dense, needlelike foliage

[a]O, oval; P, pyramidal; R, round; U, upright; W, weeping; V, vase-shaped; WS, wide-spreading.

Does a tree provide heavy, moderate, or light shade? Does it prefer a certain exposure, such as north? Norway maples provide heavy shade, while honey locusts give light to moderate shade and filtered views. Trees in a southern exposure may thaw in winter, causing damage to some of them. Crabapples prefer a sunny exposure, as do Austrian pines, while red maples and the Douglas fir will withstand partial shade.

Is the tree free from or easily susceptible to disease or insect damage? For instance, whereas the ginkgo is virtually free of pests, birches must be sprayed for leaf miner.

Form and Structure

What are the height and the spread of the tree or shrub at maturity? What is the form of the tree—round, pyramidal, oval, upright, V-shaped, wide spreading, or weeping? Is it fast or slow in growth? Red oaks grow rapidly to about 18 feet in 10 years. Some of the most rapid growers are the plane tree, 35 feet in 10 years; the green ash, over 25 feet in 10 years; and the honey locust, over 25 feet in 10 years. Is the plant deciduous or evergreen? Deciduous trees provide shade in summer and allow sunlight through in winter. Evergreen trees,

such as Carolina hemlock or Austrian pine, make good screens. Does the tree have good branch structure and bark color? A tree such as the Amur cork tree has interesting bark and branch structure for winter effect. The London plane tree has peeling bark, which adds much interest, as do stewartias.

Foliage, Flowers, and Fruit

What are the foliage size, texture, and color? The size and texture of foliage are important design qualities. Thick, heavy foliage is good for noise reduc-

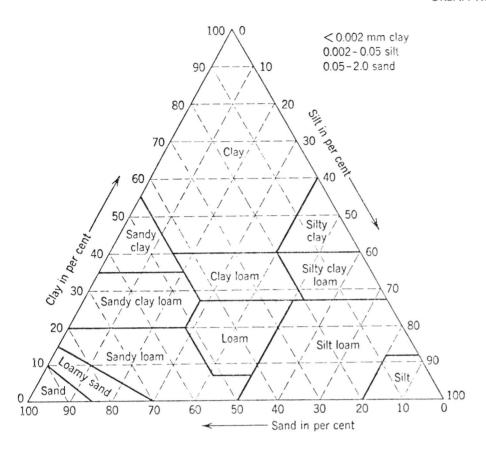

< 0.002 mm clay
0.002 – 0.05 silt
0.05 – 2.0 sand

Soil Classification Chart: U.S. Agriculture Department.

tion. Some trees have red foliage, such as the Crimson King maple or the bloodleaf Japanese maple. These trees provide added interest because of their red leaves.

Is there good autumn color? Trees with fall color are very desirable. Some examples of these are the red maple, sugar maple, red oak, pin oak, scarlet oak, dogwood, black gum, and sweet gum.

Are the flowers or fruits significant? When do they occur? Many crabapples have beautiful flowers, as well as decorative fruit. Dogwoods are also often used for their flowers, as are smaller shrubs such as azaleas.

Transplanting

Is the plant easy or difficult to transplant? Some trees, such as the scarlet oak or sweet gum, are difficult to transplant in larger sizes; others, such as the pin oak, are easily transplanted. Time of the year is also important in transplanting. For example, birches are best planted in the spring, as are magnolias.

Maintenance and Safety

Does the plant require spraying for insects or removing litter from seed pods or leaves? Trees such as birches and crabapples need to be sprayed for insect control. Other trees, such as the horse chestnut, catalpa, and native honey locust, drop seed pods or fruit. The female ginkgo has particularly obnoxious smelling fruit, and the male variety should be chosen.

Is the plant weak wooded, is it easily susceptible to insects or disease, or does it have thorns? Trees that tend to split in windy conditions are undesirable along streets, and there may be an ordinance against their use in some cities. An example is the silver maple, which is weak wooded and prone to damage in storms. A few trees, such as hawthorns and native honey locusts, have thorns, which may cause problems. Thornless and seedless varieties of honey locust that are also resistant to disease are available.

Some evergreen trees will grow in some cities, but where industrial

pollution is high they may not survive because of particulates that remain on the leaves for more than 1 year, interfering with growth.

URBAN TREE PLANTING NEEDS AND PROCEDURES

Tree Pits

The root zone of a tree is a critical area that needs special attention if a tree is to survive and to do reasonably well under the stress of urban conditions. Tree root areas often have to contend with utilities, building or vault foundations, soil compaction, and poor drainage. Above grade, urban trees have more severe climatic effects from sunlight, reflected heat from paving, wind, temperature, and humidity, etc. Tree pits have often been confined to a small area about 4 × 4 feet with a depth of about 3 feet. This does not permit adequate soil volume for the typical street tree and only allowed about six gallons of available water at any time. Intercon-

**Tree planting detail
for trees in open
lawn areas.**

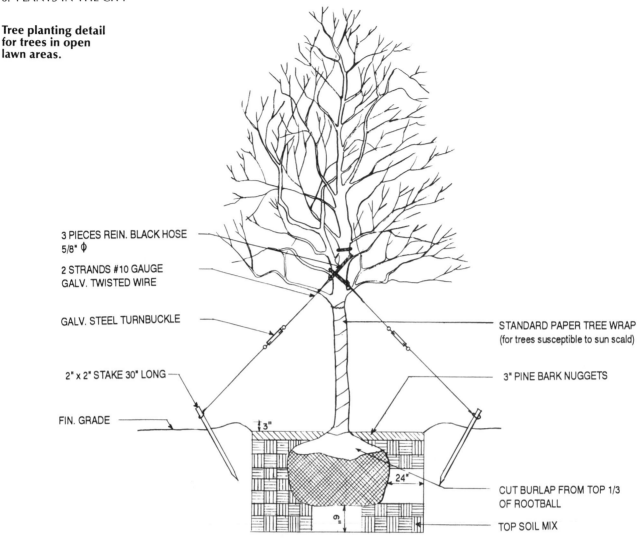

3 PIECES REIN. BLACK HOSE
5/8" Φ

2 STRANDS #10 GAUGE
GALV. TWISTED WIRE

GALV. STEEL TURNBUCKLE

2" x 2" STAKE 30" LONG

FIN. GRADE

STANDARD PAPER TREE WRAP
(for trees susceptible to sun scald)

3" PINE BARK NUGGETS

CUT BURLAP FROM TOP 1/3
OF ROOTBALL

TOP SOIL MIX

3"

24"

6"

nected tree pits or continuous tree pits that contain larger volumes of soil beneath paved areas promote balanced root growth on opposite sides of the tree. Tree islands with groups of plantings are also much better for tree growth and health. Trees planted in a minimum of 200 cubic feet of soil stay in better condition. This volume of soil allows more available water for the tree as it grows larger. A tree about 30–35 feet high with a 10-foot crown radius needs about 300 cubic feet of soil at a 3-foot depth in the northeast with, for example, 15 percent water-holding capacity for a 10-day period between rainfalls. The amount of soil varies with the region of the country and, in Denver, a similar tree would require 700 cubic feet of soil. Larger trees have even greater needs of up to 1000 cubic feet or more of soil. Soil volume can be

calculated based on the trees canopy size and pan evaporation rates for different cities, which is available from the National Oceanographic and Atmospheric Administration (NOAA).

To allow water runoff to reach tree roots, unit pavers are semipermeable and allow more water for tree roots than concrete paving. Unit pavers permit water to percolate through jointing material. Permeable material such as course bitumen-bound sand works well. A geotextile mat below the pavers may help reduce compaction. A raised curb around planting can help with compaction, and perforated capped aeration pipes can also help. Where a base course in adjacent paving is needed slag (8–15 cm) may be used and allows better percolation even when compacted than gravel. If sandy soil is mixed

with slag at 2 parts slag to 1 part soil less layering will occur below the base course.

Soil Composition

Soil is composed of mineral and organic matter, water, and air. Three mineral particles and one organic particle affect soil texture. Sand is the largest (0.05–2.0 mm) mineral particle. Sand increases aeration and drainage but has little moisture holding capacity. Silt, a smaller (0.002–0.05 mm) particle increases moisture holding capacity, and clay, the smallest soil particle (0.002 mm and smaller), increases nutrient holding capacity. Organic matter averages 3 to 5 percent in topsoil, and it keeps soil loose and porous. A sandy loam will be about 60 percent sand, 25 percent silt, and 15 percent clay.

Soil Tests

Topsoil must be tested at a laboratory for pH. Where necessary, the acidity or alkalinity range of the soil required by a plant must be adjusted. The pH scale extends from 0 to 14, with a pH value of 7 being neutral, below 7 acidic, and above 7 alkaline. The pH scale is logarithmic, and changing from pH 7 to pH 8 means 10 times more alkaline, while going from pH 6.5 to pH 4.5 means that the soil is 100 times more acidic. Most plants need a pH of 6 to 6.5. Some plants, such as the red oak, however, will grow in a more acidic soil with a pH of 5.5 or less. Soil pH is also important because it is related to nutrient availability. Plants absorb nutrients from the soil in liquid form. Nutrients are most readily available in soil with a nearly neutral pH.

Soil can also be tested for organic content and required nutrients—nitrogen, potassium, phosphorus, and trace elements such as manganese and iron.

A typical soil mix for planting areas would be 80 percent topsoil and 20 percent coarse sand. The soil mix should not be too sandy or water-holding capacity will be reduced. Drainage lines should be placed in the bottom of continuous tree pits, and in smaller areas where problem areas exist.

Planting and Guying

A tree is generally dug at the nursery with an earth ball, which is burlapped and tied with rope to keep it from breaking. When the tree is planted, the topsoil should be no higher than the tree was when growing at the nursery. This would be a few inches above the burlapped ball. After the tree is planted, it should be well watered to remove air pockets in the soil. A tree is guyed to prevent movement of the tree from breaking the earth ball or from being blown over by wind. Galvanized steel guy wires are placed through rubber hose and fastened around the tree. They are then tied to stakes or deadmen placed in the ground, eyelets fastened to

sidewalk blocks, or cedar stakes placed vertically adjacent to the tree. Turnbuckles are often used to tighten guy wires, but are generally not needed. The guy wires should be removed after two years.

Wrapping

After the tree is planted, the trunk may be wrapped with paper tree wrap or good quality burlap up to the first major branch. The purpose of the tree wrap is to prevent sun scald of some species, such as sugar maple. The trunk should be inspected for wounds or insect damage before the tree is wrapped. In most cases it has been found that tree wrap is not necessary and may cause damage if the rope holding the tree wrap in place is not removed as the tree grows.

Pruning

Pruning the newly planted tree helps keep the evaporation of water in balance with the retention capacity of the roots, which have been cut back to the root ball. Depending on the form and structure of the tree, about one-third of the branches should be cut back.

Mulch

Generally, after the tree is guyed and watered, a mulch of peat moss or wood chips about 3 inches deep is applied from the trunk of the tree to the edge of the excavation to help the root system retain moisture.

Saucer

A saucer about 3 inches high is then created around the tree to retain moisture after watering.

Planting Dates

Planting dates vary with the local seasons and the type of tree. Some trees do better when planted in the spring. These trees, if deciduous, should be planted before the new leaves come out. If trees are balled

before the leaves come out, they may be stored until ready for planting. After leaves develop, special precautions must be taken when moving the trees, and there is a high chance that losses will occur. Deciduous trees can also be moved in the fall after the first hard frost.

Evergreen trees can be planted in the spring or late summer. They should be moved in the spring before new growth progresses, or at the end of the summer when new growth has hardened, temperatures have cooled, and the soil is of proper consistency for digging the earth balls. This is usually the end of August to the middle of September. Evergreens generally prefer acidic soil, and organic materials such as peat moss are added to the topsoil.

Maintenance

When trees are planted in the city, they need care in the form of pruning, watering, fertilizing, and spraying to prevent fungus or insect damage. Tree grates help in allowing rain water to reach the tree while preventing compaction of soil by pedestrians. The tree grate should be designed or selected to be expandable in size to allow room for the tree to grow without injury. Brick or granite pavers with oversize joints are often better than tree grates, however, using just mulch often works best. Problems from snow removal must also be considered. If chemicals are used, sodium nitrate is preferred instead of sodium or calcium chloride.

Trees can be raised above sidewalk areas by means of curbs or raised tree planters. If raised tree planters are used, winter injury to the roots of plants in the containers may be a problem. Roots are more sensitive to low temperatures than are upper portions of a plant. Insulation on the walls of the planter may help prevent injury to the roots. Raised planters must also have good drainage and, when used on rooftop areas, must contain drains. The drain usually has about 3 inches of gravel above it and is separated from the topsoil mix by a fiberglass mat.

View of streetscape treatment at Sparks Street Mall, Ottawa, Ontario, Canada. (Photograph by Ewald Richter).

7

Pedestrian Mall Case Studies

To examine in depth the design features and development strategies of malls, case studies of full malls, semi-malls, and transit malls are presented in this chapter. These examples provide an overview of malls that have been built in the United States and Canada in the past 33 years and how they have evolved. During this period (as now) many central city retail areas needed to be revitalized in order to survive and to compete with suburban shopping centers. There were problems such as traffic congestion, pollution, lack of adequate parking, and deterioration of buildings and the economic base in many downtowns.

These factors, as well as the desire to provide a pleasant environment for urban shoppers, led to the development of malls in many cities, beginning in Kalamazoo, Michigan, in 1959. Many of these malls have features such as fountains, sculpture, new paving, planting, sitting areas, children's play areas, night lighting, and comfort stations, and are centers for promotional and cultural events.

These malls have been financed in a variety of ways by Federal Urban Renewal Agency funds; by assessment districts; by the city, county, and state; by the Urban Mass Transportation Administration; by Community Development Program Funds; by private business associations; and by other programs as funds become available.

Providing a pleasant environment for retail sales (including good access, transit, and parking) may increase investor confidence and spur new construction in the downtown and broaden the tax base. Several of the malls have been successful at reversing the decline of retail sales in the downtowns and have encouraged pedestrian use by providing separation of vehicular and pedestrian circulation and improved transit, or by expanding walks creating a quality urban streetscape with amenities and activities that attract people. Other malls built in the 1970s began after new suburban shopping areas were constructed and did not get an early enough start to adequately compete. Further factors are discussed in Chapter 8.

Full Malls and Combination Semimalls

Oldtown Mall

Baltimore, Maryland

Description

Oldtown Mall is a full mall located in Baltimore, Maryland, a city with a population of 751,400. The Oldtown area is historically significant and is the site of one of the three original settlements that combined to become the city of Baltimore. The mall is located on the 400 and 500 blocks of Gay Street for a length of about 1500 feet. The mall removes traffic from an area that was formerly choked with automobile and service trucks. Pedestrians had used narrow sidewalks and experienced difficult circulation on the crowded street.

The mall has a width of 45 feet and features a fountain, new brick paving, sitting areas, planting, and night light-ing. Buildings along the mall have also been renovated as part of the renewal plan with the intention of recapturing the rich architectural qualities of these nineteenth century buildings. Architects for the mall were O'Malley and Associates, Inc., and the landscape architect was William H. Potts. Oldtown Mall was financed by Federal Urban Renewal Agency funds and Community Development Program block grant funds. The mall was completed in 1976 at a cost of $2.6 million.

Development Strategy

The primary purpose of the mall was the revitalization of the Gay Street shopping area, which began to develop in 1813, when the Belair Market was established at the edge of town on Gay Street. In the 1880s this was the downtown of Baltimore. Since the 1940s the shopping area and residential neighborhoods gradually declined, and by 1960 Gay Street served low-income black residents of public housing projects and adjacent neighborhoods picked for urban renewal. Assessed valuation dropped by 18 percent between 1963 and 1968, and more vacant stores and marginal businesses appeared.

Merchants petitioned assistance from the city and were included in an urban renewal program that comprised a project area of 35 blocks under the Department of Housing

Plan of mall. (Photograph courtesy of O'Malley and Associates, Inc.)

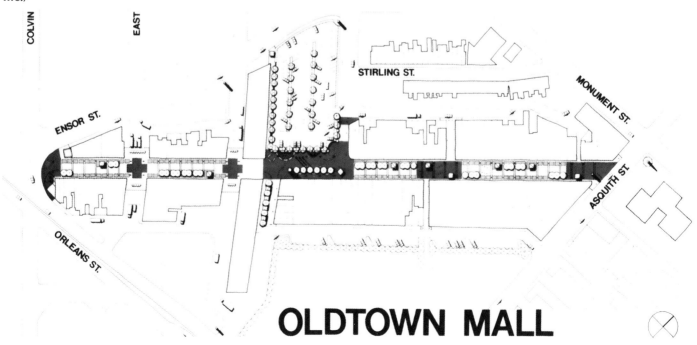

OLDTOWN MALL

and Urban Development. In 1968 the Oldtown Project was initiated, and a tenuous alliance was formed between the black residential community, represented by a Model Cities Council, and the predominantly white merchants. The merchants appointed one member to represent it on the council. The city's community organizers and planners were important in maintaining the coalition. When special meetings were held with the merchants on rehabilitation standards, residents were always invited. Planning was carried out through biweekly community meetings over the period of 1 year.

The Oldtown Plan was adopted by the City Council through an ordinance that included mandatory rehabilitation standards. The plan called for the following:

1. Metered off-street parking areas in locations formerly occupied by commercial buildings.
2. Conversion of Gay Street into a shopping mall, and the rerouting of through traffic around the shopping area.
3. Mandatory rehabilitation of existing stores in accordance with city codes and special exterior standards. Financial assistance through HUD 312 loans was a major factor in securing the acceptance of rehabilitation requirements.
4. Redevelopment of the surrounding neighborhood for new housing, parks, and public facilities.

At the time the rehabilitation effort was to be started, the HUD 312 loan funds (3 percent for 20 years) were held up but eventually became available. Also, the Small Business Administration 502 Program was used.

The architectural consultant carried out a planning study to direct and assist the owners and tenants of commercial properties in the renovation program.

The renewal ordinance called for buildings to be restored to their original architectural character on upper floors. Flat signs on buildings are limited to the bottom of the second-story window or 13 feet above grade. Projecting signs may be no more than 7 feet beyond the building and no higher than 13 feet, or lower than 10 feet, above grade, with a maximum size of 4 square feet. Lettering identifying the business may be applied to ground floor show windows but may be no more than 2.5 inches in height.

Stores with new signs conforming to the sign control program and with newly renovated facades began to appear along Gay Street. After some merchants began their rehabilitation efforts, others followed, and nearly 100 percent of the owners cooperated, with the rehabilitation to be completed by the time the mall was opened.

The city's off-street parking commission provided metered lots on sites cleared through urban renewal. Although the low fees will probably not generate adequate funds to repay the cost of operation and debt service, the subsidy can be justified on the basis that taxes from stores are increased by the provision of parking spaces.

Design Features

FOUNTAIN

In one area of the mall called Oldtown Square, several buildings have been removed and the mall has been widened to 70 feet. This area contains a fountain with adjacent sitting areas and is one of the focal points of the mall. The fountain has

View of fountain.

several aerated jets and an interesting texture on the base of washed river gravel set in concrete, surrounded by brick steps. This square also features a clock tower and performance area.

PAVING

Paving is predominantly brick in different patterns, and in Oldtown Square circular concrete bands are used as part of the paving pattern in conjunction with round tree grates.

BENCHES

Benches are made of concrete and are curved to act as sculptural elements.

PLANTING

Trees are planted both in walk areas and in raised round redwood planters or tubs.

NIGHT LIGHTING

The lights are clear round globes on metal poles at pedestrian scale, and there are also spotlights on higher poles to highlight various features of the mall.

In Retrospect

Along with development of the mall, storefronts have been rehabilitated with new signs conforming to the sign control program. Also, it appears that property values along the mall have increased since completion of the project. Black ownership of businesses has also increased from about 10 to 30 percent as a result of federal loan programs.

The area has maintained its profile of independently owned merchandise, apparel, and specialty establishments and has experienced gains in service establishments. There has been no increase in restaurants and no apparent increase in employees in the businesses that stayed on the mall. The mall is considered to be moderately successful.

**Brick paving with
circular tree grates.**

**Lighting and round
redwood planters.**

Michigan Mall

Battle Creek, Michigan

Description

Michigan Mall is located in Battle Creek, Michigan, a city with 53,500 residents, 100 miles west of Detroit. The mall was developed to revitalize the downtown shopping area. Michigan Mall covers four blocks, including one cross block at Madison Street. It stretches along the city's primary artery from Carlyle Street to City Hall at Division Street. The landscape architects for the mall were Johnson, Johnson, and Roy, Inc. and traffic planners were Harland Bartholomew. The right-of-way is generally 72 feet. The block at the center of the mall, McCamly to Capital is completely closed to traffic, and the blocks at either end are of the semimall type.

The mall features fountains, sculpture, overhead trellis areas, new paving, a clock tower, display areas, lighting, sitting areas, and planting. The Michigan Mall was funded by special assessment, the city, and a private grant. The mall was completed in June 1975, at a cost of $2 million.

Development Strategy

In 1959 the concept of a mall was discussed by the merchants in Battle Creek. The merchants considered urban renewal but decided not to pursue this method for revitalization of the downtown. Funding from the Department of Housing and Urban Development was applied for but was not granted. Eventually, the association of Retail Businessmen hired a design consultant to develop a plan for the downtown.

This plan was funded by a special assessment of the 250 businesses for 45 percent of its cost, by the city for 45 percent, and by a private grant from the Miller Foundation for 10 percent.

Design Features

The design concept allows for easy pedestrian circulation from one side of the street to the other and the relation of commercial or civic functions to the spaces created.

FOUNTAINS
The plaza facing Civic Theatre has a fountain-sculpture as a focal point. There is also a water feature plaza with a sunken pool and bubbler fountain.

PAVING
The paving on the mall is brick and concrete.

CLOCK TOWER
The major display plaza has a central clock tower built on a concrete structure.

TRELLIS
There is a garden display plaza that has an overhead trellis area. Gas lighting is used in this area.

SITTING AREA
There are several types of sitting areas. Some benches are built into raised planters or walls, while others are free standing.

RAISED PLANTERS
Planters help define many of the spaces and form the edge of fountains

Plan of the mall. (Photograph courtesy of the Planning Department of Battle Creek.)

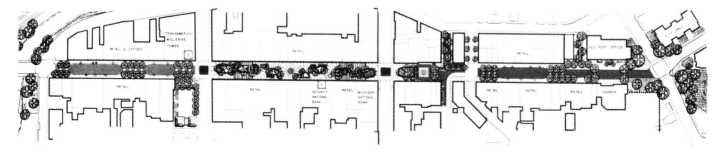

and other features. They are made of concrete.

LIGHTING

Night lighting in some areas is provided by gas-lit fixtures. In other areas metal standards with luminaires are used.

PLANTING

A variety of trees and other plant materials is used on the mall, such as red maple, Marshall's seedless ash, redbud, cotoneaster, yews, azaleas, and flowers. The plant materials were selected for ecological compatibility with minimum maintenance.

In Retrospect

Sales of major stores increased up to 30 percent after the first year that the

mall had been opened. Pedestrian traffic has also substantially increased, but the Michigan Avenue Mall is no longer a competitive location for retail and office uses. About 16% of the existing street level retail space is vacant and less than 50% is currently in retail use. The balance is occupied by office and service functions. Rent is about 40% lower than general Battle Creek market area. While the Battle Creek market is stable, it is not growing. Instead, new activity centers have developed with over one million square feet of new retail space since 1983 on the Columbia and Beckly Road corridor. The development of new office space and apartments is also following this trend of suburbanization.

Building facades facing the mall have also declined. Rear facades with

building faces oriented to streets and parking areas are kept in better condition.

The mall originally was to be complemented by a ring road one block away, but this road was never fully implemented. As a result major access through the downtown is two blocks away with little visual connection to the mall. Some trees are overgrown, which blocks views of the mall and may give the feeling of inadequate security. The full mall between McCamly to Capital has not been successful and studies are presently being conducted on options for whether the remaining block should be opened to traffic along with other renovation. Adjacent blocks of the mall are open to traffic and were designed as a semimall.

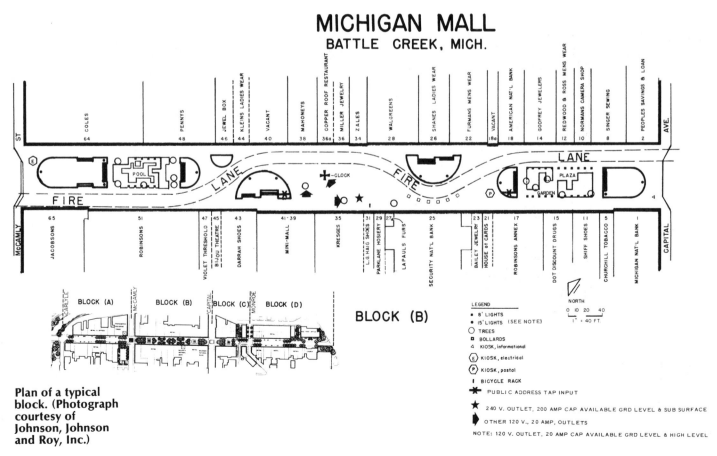

Plan of a typical block. (Photograph courtesy of Johnson, Johnson and Roy, Inc.)

Fountain with sculpture. (Photograph courtesy of Johnson, Johnson and Roy, Inc.)

Streetscape treatment with raised concrete planters. (Photograph courtesy of the Planning Department of Battle Creek.)

Clock tower.
(Photograph cour-
tesy of Johnson,
Johnson and Roy,
Inc.)

Fountain with bubbler. (Photograph courtesy of Johnson, Johnson and Roy, Inc.)

Main Street Mall

Charlottesville, Virginia

Description

The Main Street Mall is located in Charlottesville, Virginia, a city with a population of 45,010. Charlottesville has a unique historic background, being the home of Thomas Jefferson.

The mall, eight blocks in length and 60 feet in width, is the main activity center of the central business district. It was therefore the best place to start downtown revitalization with the expectation that people will use the downtown if it is a pleasant place to be: visually attractive, clean, safe, and auto-free. Design features of the mall include new paving, lighting, fountains, kiosks, seating, and planting. Landscape architects for the mall were Lawrence Halprin and Associates and economic consultants were Hammer, Siler, George, and Associates.

The first phase of the mall with five blocks was funded from the city capital improvement budget for 75 percent of its cost and from assessments of abutting property owners for 25 percent. The first phase of the mall was completed in July 1976, at a cost of $2 million. In July 1980, a second phase of the mall began with an extension of two additional blocks at a cost of $826,000. The third phase consisted of one block, which was completed in June 1985. It had a cost of approximately $800,000 and was part of a hotel and conference center development at the western end.

Location plan of the first phase of the mall.

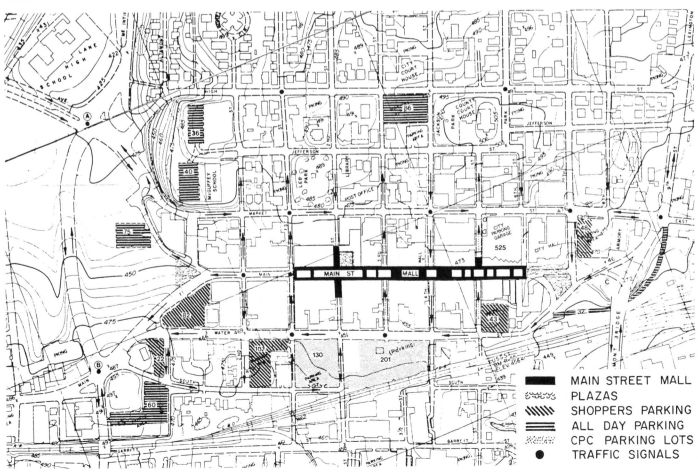

MAIN STREET MALL
PLAZAS
SHOPPERS PARKING
ALL DAY PARKING
CPC PARKING LOTS
TRAFFIC SIGNALS

Development Strategy

The idea of a mall began in 1971, when the city government decided that some action was needed to protect the tax base in the central business district. A Central City Commission made up of area residents, business people, government officials, and others was formed to determine a concept for revitalizing the downtown. Their idea was a mall.

After the design consultant was retained, a 3-day workshop involving the Central City Commission was held. Thirty-two people participated. Some of the objectives agreed on were the following:

1. The downtown retail market and its economic share should be stabilized and redefined as a specialty area with diverse commercial, cultural, and residential uses.
2. There should be pedestrian areas separated from automobiles.
3. Downtown amenities should be as good as those found in the best suburban shopping centers, or better.
4. The downtown should have many cultural and recreational features such as art, sculpture, music, and theatre.

5. Existing older buildings should be recycled and given new uses.
6. The architectural and historic character of downtown Charlottesville should be revitalized. There should be as little vehicular traffic as possible crossing the mall.
7. There should be preservation and conservation of older structures on Main Street.
8. Design control and review provisons for downtown Charlottesville should be created and enforced.

After public hearings and a great deal of public controversy, the City Council voted to proceed with funds for the mall. The above objectives were then carried out.

The overall concept of the mall included eight blocks of the pedestrian mall, Central Place with specialty shopping areas, the civic plaza on the eastern end in front of City Hall, informal open space plaza on the western end, and improvement of 12 side streets. Clockwise one-way traffic flow on two parallel streets was also provided for convenient vehicular circulation along with the provision of adequate parking.

Design Features

The design of the mall does not emphasize the linear quality of the street but instead reorganizes it into a series of outdoor rooms. These rooms, which develop in a sequence of spaces, are defined by bosques of trees numbering six to eight in double rows.

PAVING
The mall is paved in brick with concrete bands. Where intersecting streets have been closed off, concrete pavers form a pattern in the brick paving.

FOUNTAINS
These features are made of granite and provide differing water effects. Three fountains are located on the mall. Two of them are small and have water bubbling out of granite blocks in sitting areas located beneath bosques of trees. The other larger fountain forms a focus on the mall, and has granite elements with water pouring into a metal container.

FLOWER POTS
These elements, planted with junipers and flowers, add color throughout the mall.

Brick paving on the mall.

View of granite fountain.

View of main fountain.

KIOSKS

Kiosks are also used on the mall and are lighted for night effect. The kiosks contain drinking fountains.

SITTING AREAS

Sitting areas with benches are provided throughout the mall. These movable benches are located beneath bosques of trees adjacent to the larger fountain.

LIGHTING

Black metal poles with pendular clusters of four luminaires line the mall. Uplighting is also provided for trees.

PLANTING

Trees are planted in groups to define spaces and to provide shade. The trees used on the mall are willow oak and maple.

In Retrospect

The mall creates a pleasant place for a variety of activities. Shaded sitting areas, especially those with fountains, create an inviting environment for people to relax, and benches can be arranged for ease of conversation.

In the past 5 years retail sales have increased along with property values and assessed rental value. The mall has resulted in many new businesses locating in the downtown. Many private renovation activities have also resulted. Over $4.73 million of private investment occurred from July 1976 to July 1980 and over $8 million from July 1980 to 1982.

The overall objectives of the development strategy are being met. The combination of the public–private team effort with strong leadership from the City under the direction of the City Manager worked well. Significant housing improvements have also been made in the Central City area, and revitalization is proceeding on upper stories of residential structures. The mall seems to be achieving its objectives of revitalization of the downtown and is considered very successful.

Main Street is safe for pedestrians and attractive enough to encourage a variety of activities; as a result people are coming to the downtown area. The intent of the plan also was to utilize materials that are in harmony with the historic character of the city.

View of granite fountain and related sitting area.

Flower pots.

Kiosk on the mall.

Seating on the mall is very flexible, and people can group the benches for ease of conversation.

**Lights designed for
the mall reflect
incandescent light.**

**Bosques of willow
oaks are used on
the mall.**

City Center Mall

Eugene, Oregon

Description

City Center Mall is located in Eugene, Oregon, a city of 106,000 residents. It established a pedestrian precinct in a seven and one-half block area, replacing the vehicular emphasis of former city streets. These blocks included three city blocks on Broadway, three blocks on Willamette Street, and one and one-half blocks on Olive in downtown Eugene.

The existing streets for the mall have a right-of-way of 66 feet and feature the Central Plaza at Broadway and Willamette, with a fountain as its focus, new paving of brick and concrete, play areas with rest room facilities, planting, night lighting, sitting areas, and a partially covered walkway at midblock leading to parking facilities.

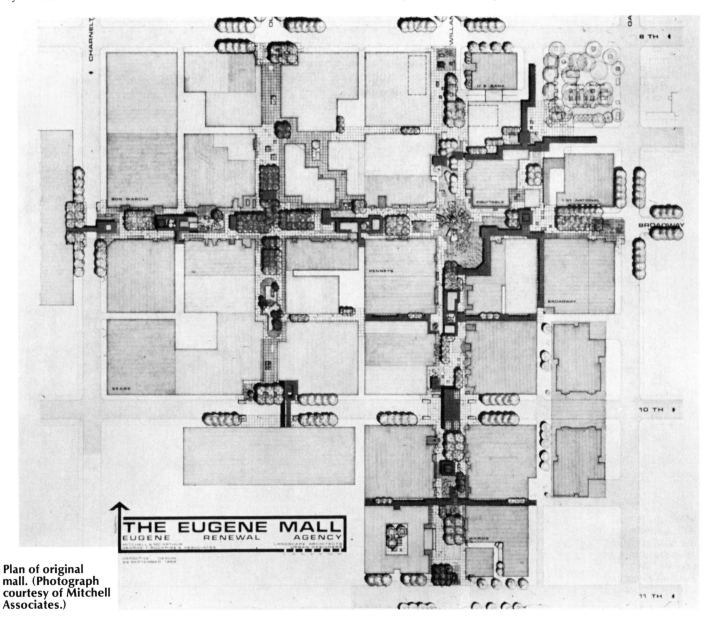

Plan of original mall. (Photograph courtesy of Mitchell Associates.)

The project was accomplished with urban renewal funds from the federal government. The first phase of the mall was completed in 1971/1972 at a cost of $1.3 million. In 1985 one block of the mall on Willamette between 10th and 11th Street was converted to vehicular traffic with streetscape amenities retained. This block also has a planted median down the center. The renovation involved the removal of a playground and a large pedestrian canopy that spanned 10th Street and connected the block with the rest of the mall. The canopy was removed because it obscured views of three historic buildings and created a dark area that attracted loiterers. Also, in 1987, two blocks were redesigned on Broadway between Charnelton and Willamette, eliminating the covered areas, renovating the children's playground, and providing new light fixtures, benches, drinking fountains, and telephone booths. Landscape architects for the original mall were

Mitchell, McArthur, Gardiner and O'Kane; architects were Morin, Longwood, and Edlund; and planners were George Rockrise and Associates.

Development Strategy

The primary objectives of the downtown renewal were to improve the area through redevelopment and rehabilitation of substandard buildings, to eliminate blight, to modify the street system, to provide adequate parking, and to create traffic-free pedestrian precincts. Also, it was believed that these improvements would stimulate private investment in new development, protect the existing economic base, and provide an increase in taxes for the city and county. Under provisions of state legislation enacted in 1957, the mayor and the City Council started the Urban Renewal Agency of Eugene. After several trips to California to review renewal projects, civic leaders

became enthusiastic about federally assisted renewal programs and began the efforts that led to the mall.

In 1965 the City Council appointed a six-member group of citizens to serve as the Eugene Development Commission. In 1967 a seventh member was added, and the commission became the Urban Renewal Agency of Eugene.

In the late 1960s the city applied for planning funds from the Department of Housing and Urban Development (HUD). Once the funds were approved, an 18-month planning effort began, involving officials, citizens, and urban planners. After public meetings the plan was adopted by the City Council in December 1968. In March 1969, the federal government approved the project.

Citizen-Community Involvement

The spring of 1966 was marked by Eugene's Conference on Community

View of the mall with banners, seating, and planting. (Photograph courtesy of City of Eugene Planning and Development Department.)

Goals, involving several hundred residents taking part in three meetings. From these meetings, statements evolved that were adopted by the City Council as the official community goals and policies.

A 100-member citizens' advisory committee (SCORE: Special Committee on Renewing Eugene) was established in October 1966. The members appointed by the mayor included businessmen, educators, professionals, tradesmen, and housewives. Meetings were held in city council chambers, and citizens were invited.

During the survey and planning phase conducted by the planning consultants SCORE met more than a dozen times. Final decisions were made by the Planning Review Committee, which consisted of seven SCORE members, the mayor and the City Council, the Eugene Planning Commission, and The Eugene Urban Renewal Agency members. The Plan-

ning Review Committee held several meetings with the architectural consultants, and all meetings were open to the public. Several subcommittees of SCORE provided advice and technical assistance in regard to historic structures, urban design, and socioeconomic concerns.

Social, Economic, and Environmental Considerations

The physical form of the mall resulted from objectives developed by the community. These objectives were as follows:

1. An attractive design unique to Eugene.
2. An attractive and competitive retail market offering a diversity of goods.
3. Separation of pedestrian and vehicular traffic.
4. Elimination of nonessential vehicular traffic.
5. Adequate parking, separate from pedestrian areas.
6. Improved public transportation service to the city center.
7. Protection from the weather for pedestrians.
8. A lively atmosphere.
9. A place of contact for all groups of the metropolitan population.
10. A mix of activities that could not flourish in other locations.

Design Features

FOUNTAINS
Central Plaza at Broadway and Willamette is the focal point of the mall and serves as a gathering place. It has a water feature consisting of 37 concrete elements, the highest of which is 25 feet. Water cascades over the blocks into a series of pools at a rate of 3400 gallons a minute. The fountain invites pedestrians to walk through it or sit on its concrete walls. A second-level viewing platform is at

Bosque of trees with tree grates and guards integrated into the paving pattern.

the southeast corner of the plaza. The fountain is intended to symbolize the mountains and streams of Oregon.

A landscaped plaza at Broadway and Olive has a circular water feature, which serves as the focal point for a more intimate plaza, oriented to quiet activities. It has sitting areas and also contains small game tables with built-in checker boards.

PLAY AREA
A play area on Broadway stimulates creative play and has adjacent rest rooms. It was renovated in 1987.

PAVING AND MATERIALS
Entry areas announce the mall by means of kiosks, lawn panels, brick, bollards, and a bosque of trees. A grid paving pattern of brick and concrete is used on portions of the mall. To avoid large warped areas, there is a continuous trench drain with a brick cover.

PLANTING
Plant materials were selected to provide seasonal color, soften the harsh lines of adjacent elements, provide screening, develop spaces, and minimize maintenance. Tree grates and guards are used around trees for protection and added interest.

MALL LIGHTING
Lighting provides a warm but uneven level of illumination, making the mall an inviting place to be. Trees are up-lighted, and entrances and focal elements are also lighted, although store windows are maintained as the main light source.

SERVICE
Service to the mall is provided from courts in the center of the mall, accessible from alleys.

MAINTENANCE
Complete maintenance is provided by the Eugene Parks and Recreation Department. Lawns and landscaped areas are trimmed and irrigated and fertilized.

In Retrospect

The mall inspires favorable comments from visitors, and the majority of Eugene residents find shopping more pleasant. The mall has also generated renovation of buildings, along with new development that extends pedestrian circulation through private property. In addition, the city of Eugene, in October 1973, provided the general public with free unlimited-time parking in the downtown. The parking district comprises an area of 15 square blocks within 2 blocks of the mall. Employers and employees of businesses cannot use these lots. The cost of this program is paid for by property owners, businesses, and professionals.

The mall was originally constructed at the same time an indoor mall was opening. At one time there were five major department stores; at present only one department store remains. The two redesigned blocks on Broadway are the strongest economically with few vacancies. The block with reintroduced traffic has had over one

View of paving pattern, lighting, seating, and other mall features. (Photograph courtesy of Mitchell Associates.)

million dollars in private investment with rehabilitation of adjacent buildings.

On May 21, 1991 a city-wide election was held in which voters were asked whether or not to renovate the remaining two blocks of Willamette Street and one block of Broadway and reopen them to automobile traffic. The streets could be closed for special events. Also involved was new lighting, benches, planting similar to what was provided on the renovated block of Broadway, a pavilion in the central plaza at Broadway and Willamette with a food court and restrooms, a new fountain to replace a larger existing one, and a vest pocket park on the plaza's northeast corner.

The ballot measure to renovate the three blocks and open them to traffic was not advisory and was defeated by a majority of 54 to 46 percent. Although the ballot did not authorize any spending, the overall project cost was estimated at $3.2 million. Fans of the mall felt it could be renovated more easily and in a less costly manner than the proposal by the city, and that it could be done without lifting the ban on motor vehicle traffic on the pedestrian-oriented blocks.

Apparently, even though the ballot measure was not approved, there is a consensus that the remaining two blocks of Willamette Street and one block of Broadway can use some updating of the design of the streetscape treatment, such as removal of pedestrian canopies that create dark areas. Overall, there has been a neutral feeling from the city on the success of the mall. It has helped improve the attractiveness of the downtown, however, it has not helped bring people into the city after working hours, and there has not been an increase in rental or property values.

Fulton Mall

Fresno, California

Description

Fulton Mall is located in Fresno, California, a city with a population 307,090. Fresno is part of the St. Joaquin Valley between Los Angeles and San Francisco. The mall is six blocks in length and creates a pedestrian area free of automobile traffic. Traffic is banned also from two streets crossing the mall, providing pedestrians with 0.5 mile of uninterrupted walks.

The mall features concrete paving with red pebbled bands, fountains, reflecting pools, arbors, sitting areas, children's play areas, sculpture, night lighting, and adjacent parking facilities. The architect for the mall was Victor Gruen Associates and the landscape architects were Eckbo, Dean, and Williams. The project was accomplished by creating an assessment district and by using Federal Urban Renewal Agency funds. The mall, which cost $1.6 million, was dedicated in September 1964.

Development Strategy

The primary purpose of the mall was to revitalize the downtown, beginning with Fulton Street, a traditional shopping street congested with traffic.

In 1956 Sears, Roebuck moved out of the downtown to a suburban location. This action spurred merchants to take the initiative to improve the retail district. The Fresno Redevelopment Agency was created in 1956. The Fresno Hundred Percenters, now called the Downtown Association, provided an organization of businessmen and property owners supporting renewal. In 1958 the city, the Redevelopment Agency, and the Downtown Association hired a planning consultant.

Planning the mall and overall superblock of 85 acres involved many groups. Among them were the California Highway Department, the county, the Civic Center Committee, the Convention Bureau, bus lines, the Trucking Association, the League of Women Voters, the American Institute of Architects, and federal agencies, as well as the city government.

To finance the mall, the Pedestrian Mall Act of 1960 was enacted by the state legislature. This act enabled main streets in commercial areas to be restricted and improved for pedestrian use. Costs of development could be assessed against the lands benefited or could be financed with other funds available to the city, including urban renewal funds.

Planning Considerations

The major planning objectives for revitalizing the retail district were the following:

1. To treat the center city as a core superblock that is pedestrian oriented.
2. To provide peripheral parking in multistory garages surrounding the superblock.
3. To study freeway routes and circulation around core areas.

Design Features

FREEWAY ROUTES
Freeway routes were established 20 years ahead of their construction, and the triangular freeway system was designed to provide a loop around the 1500-acre core.

PAVING
The paving is formed of concrete with curvilinear bands of red pebbles imported from Mexico. The concrete

was sandblasted and treated with an epoxy coating.

FOUNTAINS
The mall was designed with many water features, including cascades, pools, and jets. Sculptures are also part of some of the fountains.

PLANTING
Plant materials include 162 trees and 19,000 plants, giving much variety. The trees provide canopies of shade along the mall.

SITTING AREAS
Seating is provided on benches, as well as under trellised areas and around fountains, for many people.

SCULPTURE
Sculpture has been provided by a citizens' group, which has raised over $150,000 for works of art. These art objects are numerous throughout the mall. An element that serves as a landmark is a large sculptural clock toward the center of the mall (see p. 137).

MALL LIGHTING
Lighting is provided by round globes on metal standards. Some outdoor cafes and children's play areas are also features of the design that add a variety of activities.

In Retrospect

The Fulton Mall District has a very dynamic history. The mall and 323 parking spaces were completed as the first step in renewing the downtown. From the late 1960s into the early 1970s, the mall stores were fully occupied, there was an increase in property values, the mall acted as a catalyst for downtown development, and was considered moderately successful. Since 1971 the trends show a succession of peaks and valleys followed by a steady decline since the mid-1980s.

The original economic premise that the Fulton Mall area could continue as the primary regional retail center of a six county trade area was misleading and not based on a true forecast of future economic trends, or adequate imagination of how future

trends could reshape the life-styles of Central Valley residents. Over the years the basic premise in the economic forecast was proven wrong, and more modern retail centers were developed in outlying market areas and within the suburban Fresno market area. In numerous instances, decentralization of retail demand away from the Fulton Mall occurred when the major retail department

stores headquartered there opened stores in other locations outside downtown Fresno.

A key premise of the Gruen Central Area Plan of 1500 acres was the development of surrounding residential neighborhoods. Despite substantial effort, less than 20 percent of the Central Area's needs for new inner-city housing development were met. The suburbanization process has

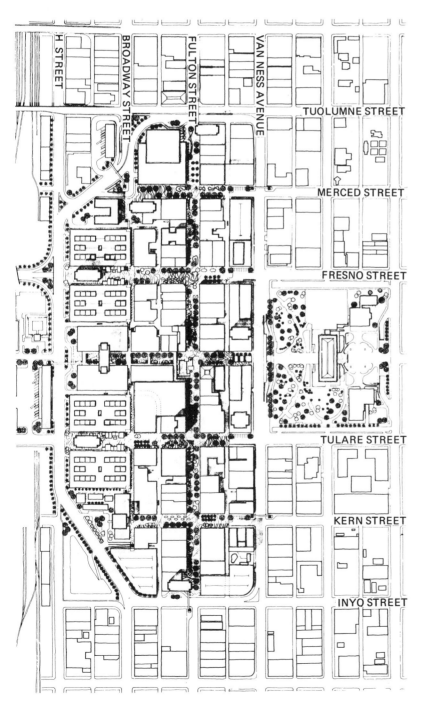

Plan of Fulton Mall.

been diminishing the Central Area of its market for several decades and has been accelerating in recent years.

The new concept for the Fulton Mall District, as provided in the recently adopted 1989 Central Area Community Plan, emphasizes specialty commercial, office, and residential uses rather than the regional commercial center that the original Gruen Plan envisioned. The plan was not carried out in the following areas:

1. The circulation scheme involving an 85-acre Superblock to be encircled by a high-speed, one-way arterial street never fully functioned because Fresno and Tulare Streets were not closed.

2. An important incentive for new investments was the provision of ample parking in advance of actual demand. The parking facilities were to be provided in major parking garages on the perimeter of the Super-

block. This would have provided easy access as well as an image of the area as a complex connected by uninterrupted pedestrian spaces. This was only partially implemented with three major parking garages along Van Ness Avenue, but the interim surface parking lots along Broadway were never replaced with the proposed parking garages.

3. The area within the Superblock never functioned as the primary

Overall view of mall, showing paving and other features. (Photograph courtesy of Gruen Associates.)

regional retail center of a six county trade area. In spite of a nationwide marketing effort, the additional major department stores were not developed in the central and north sections of the mall. Only in the south section were the major stores envisioned by the Gruen Plan accomplished. Since the regional retail concept did not work, the Redevelopment Plan was amended in 1978 with a more flexible emphasis on office/commercial projects. The marketing efforts of the Redevelopment Agency

since its absorption into City Government in 1976 have been reduced.

Business and commerce has been moving away from Fulton Street. Office vacancy is 30 percent. By the early 1980s one of the major shopping centers three miles away was remodeled and expanded, which created heavy competition for the Fresno stores. In 1989, the last major department store had left the downtown. The downtown's strength is bound in conventions and govern-

ment with retail facilities of less importance. Recently the downtown has been updated with money allocated for management and there is now a chance of turning the mall area around economically. The downtown also has an important cultural role on a regional basis for major events such as the International Exposition, Celebration of the Arts, and Cinco de Mayo. Since Fulton Mall has unique urban qualities it will be maintained as a full pedestrian mall.

View of mall. (Photograph courtesy of Gruen Associates.)

Fountain with coping for sitting.

Stone sculpture.

Metal sculpture.

Fountain with back-
drop of planting.

Fort Street Mall

Honolulu, Hawaii

Description

The Fort Street Mall is located in downtown Honolulu, Hawaii, a city of 376,110 residents. The mall is five blocks (1738 feet) in length, extending from Queen Street to Beretania Street. It averages 50 feet in width, but at the King Street Plaza it widens to 88 feet and at Father Damien Plaza Beretania Street becomes 93 feet wide. There are cross streets at Hotel and Merchant with a pedestrian underpass at King Street. The mall features include two pools, fountains, a waterfall, planters, a children's sandbox, four archways to support flowering vines, night lighting, and a special mural in the King Street underpass. The architect for the mall was Victor Gruen Associates. The project was funded by the city and county for 55 percent of the total, by private property owners for 44 percent, and by the Board of Water Supply for 1 percent. Mall construction began in June 1968, and was completed by February 1969, at a cost of $2.7 million.

Development Strategy

In the late 1940s a few individuals foresaw the decline of downtown Honolulu and made proposals to ensure its position as the center of retail and business activity in the area.

In 1949 the Hawaii Chapter of the American Institute of Architects made the first proposal to close Fort Street to vehicular traffic. For 7 years no action was taken, even though the downtown area was declining as the center of retail activity. Traffic congestion, inadequate parking, and competition from suburban shopping centers continued to drain business from the downtown. When plans were announced in 1957 for the construction of the giant Ala Moana complex, merchants feared a mass exodus by large retail establishments to the suburbs. In response to this threat the Downtown Improvement Association was formed in 1958. The association's first action was to have a master plan developed for the downtown, and its members raised $90,000 for this purpose. Master plans were provided by several different planning experts, and two different approaches emerged. This tended to confuse the direction of the project, and little was accomplished for a 6-year period. A test was carried out in July 1961, however, when Fort Street was closed for the Golden Harvest Celebration. A majority of merchants were happy with the results, and expected traffic jams did not occur. Similar events took place over the next year, and the merchants considered them successful.

In 1962, in an effort to achieve an acceptable master plan, the Downtown Improvement Association commissioned a new study. The consultant came up with a plan that provided a third approach to the downtown, resulting in more controversy.

By 1963 the downtown merchants were feeling the effects of the opening of the Ala Moana Center, and their sales dropped from $64 million, or 15 percent of the city's total, to $55 million, or 9 percent of the total.

Eventually, after the City Planning Commission presented still another approach to the downtown in 1965, the firm of Victor Gruen Associates was commissioned in 1966 to develop a plan. The firm carried out an urban design study that showed that a mall on Fort Street would be desirable. The plan called for the downtown to be divided into a series of superblocks within which a system of pedestrian malls would be developed.

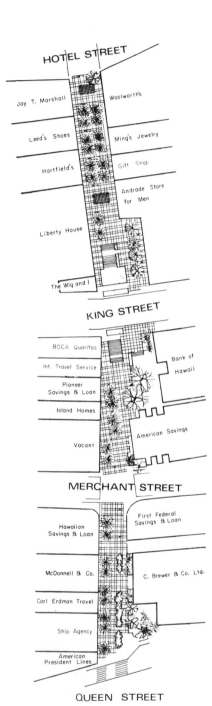

In January 1968, the City Council approved the mall after 75 percent of adjoining owners indicated their consent, and $2.4 million was budgeted for construction. Two parcels of land were purchased along Fort Street, one at King Street and the other, owned by Our Lady of Peace Cathedral, at Beretania Street. This land was needed to create a larger plaza at each end of the mall. New buildings such as the Bank of Hawaii were then set back from the mall.

Design Features

ART
The mall's major art work is a huge petroglyph mural 70 × 9 feet, cast in concrete and containing several hundred reproductions of ancient Hawaiian rock carvings. The mural is located in the King Street underpass.

The underpass was originally intended to accommodate all pedestrian circulation across King Street, but the city was petitioned by handicapped citizens to keep the on-grade crossing open.

CONCRETE ARCHWAYS
The archways were designed to act as trellises and support flowering vines. Sitting areas are provided between the archways, and many people eat their lunch there.

PAVING
The paving is concrete with brick bands in a rectilinear design.

PLANTS
Plant material includes a double row of false olive trees defining a central circulation path through the center of the mall. Other trees, such as coco palms, coral trees, bottle brush, shower trees, and monkey-pod trees, as well as numerous flowers and plants, are used for accents.

NIGHT LIGHTING
Lighting is placed on concrete piers in support trellises, as well as in planter boxes, and there are other fixtures at the underpass. A sound system is included in the overhead lighting fixtures.

FINANCIAL PLAZA
Also adjacent to the mall, between King and Merchant Streets, is the new Financial Plaza, containing the Bank of Hawaii Building, American Savings and Loan Building, and the Castle and Cooke Building. The construction cost of this project was $17 million, and it was completed in 1969.

View of mall from King Street underpass.

In Retrospect

Since completion of the mall, the decline of sales in the stores has stopped. When the mall was completed, new buildings worth $59 million were under construction. Several high rise office buildings in the downtown were constructed, and two major condominium apartment projects adjacent to the head of the mall were built. All major retail stores along the mall have remained.

Also, in 1971 Fort Street was privately extended one short block between Queen Street and Nimitz Highway to link with the AMFAC office buildings. This has improved pedestrian circulation.

The mall is now also crossed by a transit mall, which increased the number of people coming to the area. Although the mall is not in a high tourist area in relation to other parts of Honolulu, the mall has been successful. The largest department store has recently been renovated and there are some large office buildings located adjacent to the mall such as the Pacific Trade Center.

View of concrete archway, lighting, and planting.

Sitting area

Ithaca Commons

Ithaca, New York

Description

Ithaca Commons is located in Ithaca, New York, a city with a population of 28,732. The mall establishes a pedestrian plaza for two blocks on State Street and one block on Tioga Street. The mall is 66 feet wide and 1100 feet long.

The mall features a fountain, covered pavilions, a children's play area, a small amphitheatre area, sitting areas, raised planters, paving of concrete and brick, bicycle parking, planting of deciduous and evergreen trees, shrubs, and flowers, and night

Mall in relation to downtown context. (Photographs courtesy of Anton J. Egner and Associates.)

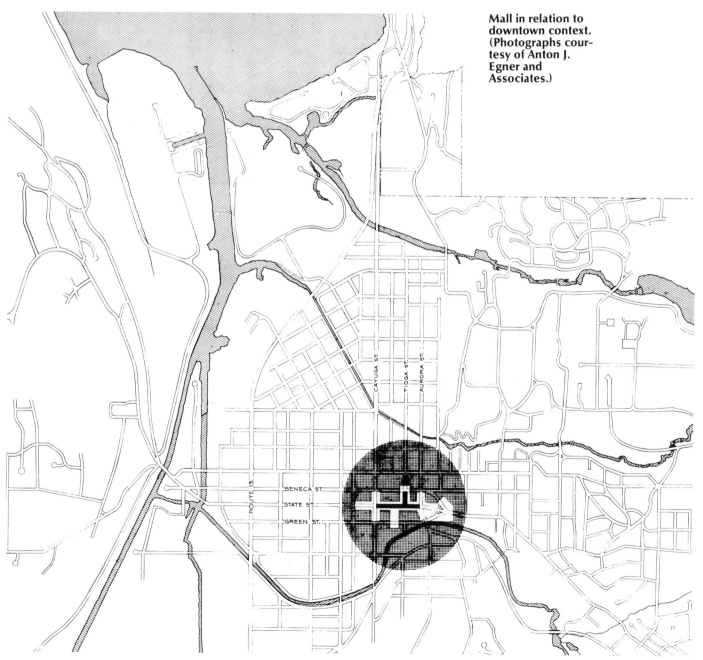

lighting. Building facades along the mall have also been improved, and parking facilities adjacent to the mall added. The architect for the mall was Anton J. Egner and Associates, and the landscape architect was Marvin Adleman. The total cost was about $1.13 million, with 85 percent provided by private property owners and 15 percent by the city. The mall was completed in August, 1975.

Development Strategy

The mall concept was presented in 1958 by the Greater Ithaca Planning Board in response to deterioration of the downtown. In the early 1960s two urban renewal plans indicated that the mall concept was important to this goal, but no progress was made until January 1972. At that time a Citizens Action Committee for a Downtown Mall was appointed by the mayor. The committee included representatives from the Downtown Businessmen's and Businesswomen's Associations and the Area Beautification Council. Each business owner on the proposed mall was spoken to personally. In addition, a public hearing was held in March 1973, to hear questions from representatives of community members.

In June 1973, the Action Committee grew into the Mall Steering Committee, and additional members were added, including other merchants, the mayor, the planning director, and members from the Planning Board and Common Council. This committee was then responsible for the planning and development of the mall. A traffic study was carried out, and data showed that from a traffic standpoint the mall was feasible. The city then committed itself to providing 900 additional parking spaces in two structures adjacent to the mall.

When a survey of merchants made in 1973 indicated that 80 percent supported the mall idea, the decision to proceed was made. About 5 percent of the merchants opposed the project, but when one business sought a court injunction to stop construction, the city won the case. The mall involved no federal funds but required an amendment to New York State's Local Finance Law to permit 20-year bonding. In order to tax the property owners, a benefit assessment district was established. There are both a primary and a secondary district. The primary district fronts on the mall, and the secondary district taxes properties within 250 feet of the mall. The tax on properties in the secondary district decreases with their distance from the end points of the mall as measured from the centerline of their frontage.

Construction on the mall was started in June 1974. In December 1974, the mayor appointed a nine-person advisory board to set guidelines for common activities and to make recommendations for improvements to adjacent buildings. The board formulated an ordinance to regulate common activities, which was adopted by the Common Council on May 7, 1975.

The advisory board also had a Commons Design Advisory Team. This organization contacted all owners and merchants about improvement of their buildings. Buildings have been sandblasted or painted, false fronts on second stories removed, and signs improved.

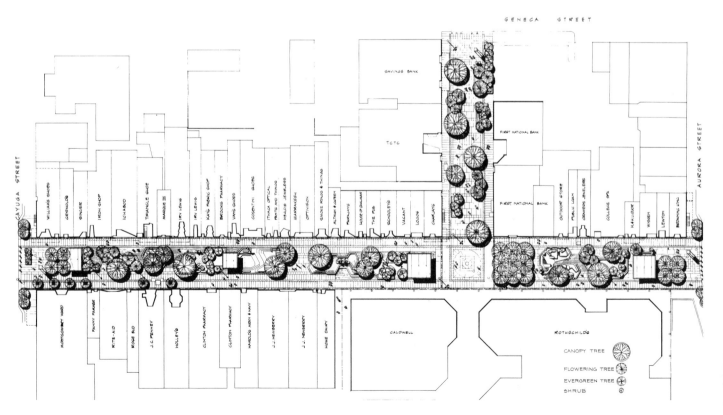

Plan of mall.

Design Features

The design concept for the mall stresses flexibility to allow a wide variety of activities, both planned and spontaneous.

FOUNTAIN
One of the features of the mall is a fountain with elements made of granite. The fountain also acts as a sculpture and symbolizes a typical gorge in New York State, where streams flow over bedrock and provide a waterfall effect.

CHILDREN'S PLAY AREA
The play area has wooden play structures, sliding boards, a chinning bar, and poles to slide down set in pea gravel in a space defined by walls and paving with a backdrop of pine trees.

PAVING
Paving of major circulation paths is concrete with brick used in major activity areas. A brick band is also placed along the low sitting walls and is expanded into the niches where benches are set back from the main walks. Ramps for the disabled are also part of the paving design of the mall.

RAISED PLANTERS
Planters with concrete walls define activity areas, some having benches integrated into the planters. The height of the planter walls also allows casual seating throughout the mall.

View of State Street before the mall was developed.

COVERED PAVILIONS

Pavilions on the mall provide weather protection and shade. These structures have wooden frameworks with metal roofs that are supported by round concrete columns.

NIGHT LIGHTING

Lighting is placed on tall metal standards with other accent lighting used for feature elements. The overhead luminaires use sodium lamps.

PLANTING

Plant materials used on the mall fall into five categories: canopy trees, trees used as sculptural or focal elements, small or flowering trees, evergreen trees, and evergreen shrubs. Trees include the Halka honey locust, Bradford pear, Washington hawthorn, Radiant crabapple, and red pine. The pine trees provide a backdrop for sitting areas, enclosure, windbreaks, and green color during bleak winter months. The evergreen shrubs include compact Pfitzer juniper and dense Japanese yews. Flowers are also provided for seasonal color and are well maintained. They are planted in the raised planters throughout the mall.

In Retrospect

Since completion of the mall, sales have increased for most merchants in the mall by as much as 22 percent. The facade program, in conjunction with a sign ordinance, has been successful, and there has been a great deal of new construction in the downtown.

Much of this construction has been spurred by the mall. The mall has also received recognition for its design. In addition, parking structures adjacent to the mall have been developed. These provide 900 parking spaces with free parking for the first 45 minutes and a small nominal charge for the next 3 hours, which may be paid for by validation from merchants. Parking is heavily subsidized and was funded by the New York State Urban Development Corporation.

The mall is used most at lunch time and pedestrian traffic slows considerably after 2:30 P.M. Property values increased as did assessed rental value. The buildings along the mall are kept in good condition. In addition, the mall is considered very successful.

View of fountain.

The children's play area is a very popular feature on the mall.

Sitting area defined by raised planters.

View of Ithaca
Commons, showing
paving, raised
walls, and seating.

Washington Square

Lansing, Michigan

Description

Washington Square is located in Lansing, Michigan, a city with a population of 130,414 people. The mall creates a pedestrian plaza three blocks (1065 feet) in length along Washington Avenue and has a width of 115.5 feet. The first phase of the mall is bounded to the north by Shiawassee Street and to the south by Michigan Street.

The mall features a spacious plaza in the 200 block of Washington Avenue for outdoor sales events and festivals; other parts have reflecting pools, sculpture, fountains, children's play areas, shaded sitting areas, and night lighting. The landscape architects for the mall were Johnson, Johnson, and Roy, Inc. The mall was accomplished with funds from the Federal Urban Renewal Agency and was completed in September 1973, at a cost of $850,000.

Two additional mall areas have been developed since 1973. The Lansing Community College Campus continues for three blocks to the north utilizing abandoned Washington Avenue street right-of-way for pedestrian areas. The Community College had 22,349 students in 1990.

During 1978–1980, Washington Avenue south of Michigan Avenue was designed into four semimall areas. Three blocks had one-way traffic and parking areas. The fourth block had two-way traffic and parking meters. Sidewalks were widened and landscaped berms were provided along with street furnishings including kiosks. Currently these four blocks have the majority of the retail businesses in the central city area. The Cooley Law School is presently expanding into the third block of this area. The school plans to invest 15–20 million dollars in the downtown area over the next 10 years. The law school had 1542 students in 1990. Davenport College, which is also in the downtown, had 1512 students in 1990.

Development Strategy

The primary objectives of revitalizing downtown Lansing were to improve the tax base and to stimulate business investment by creating an inner city complex that would be convenient to use and pleasant to visit.

During the period from 1953 to 1964, tax revenues from parts of downtown Lansing dropped as much as 50 percent. There was a decline in business due to inadequate parking, deteriorating buildings, poor lighting, fire hazards, and a rising crime rate.

The mall was part of the Project One, Lansing Urban Renewal Program. Application was approved by HUD in 1963, and implementation for Project One began in February 1965. Planning studies and a design for the mall were initiated in 1971 with completion of construction in 1973.

The plans provided that all buildings be oriented in design to use of the mall. Pedestrian passageways and plazas were designed to encourage easy pedestrian access to and from parking facilities and business establishments.

The renewal program also called for construction of five municipal parking structures to hold 4000 vehicles.

Design Features

FOUNTAINS AND SCULPTURE

The mall features pools, fountains, and sculpture. A special sculpture called "Construction 150" serves as a gateway to the mall. It was developed for Lansing by artist Jose de Rivera at a cost of $90,000. Half the cost of the sculpture was financed by the National Endowment for the Arts, with the remainder paid for by private contributions.

The mall has a sunken plaza with a pool and sculpture in the 100 block. Sitting areas and canopies of trees provide shade.

Toward the center of the mall, there is a spacious plaza with space for business displays, outdoor sales events, festivals, and special activities.

PLAY AREA AND EXHIBIT AREA

A play area and an exhibit area are located in the 300 block. In the center of the exhibit area is a reflecting pool, surrounded by paving on which canvas-covered display areas may be set up. The children's play area has wood climbing structures, along with a slide, sandbox, and playhouse. The area is shaded by trees and has benches for viewers.

PAVING

Paving is concrete with brick bands, larger activity areas having additional brick paving. The pattern provides rhythm.

KIOSKS

Kiosks are part of the street furnishings and are located in two areas of the mall.

SEATING

Seating is provided at strategic locations in the mall. It is placed away from main pedestrian circulation and directed toward interesting views, such as sculpture and planting.

PLANTING

Plant materials have been carefully selected to provide shade and to filter views of vehicular traffic. Little-leaf lindens form canopies at entrances to the square, while honey locusts provide light shade for interior areas

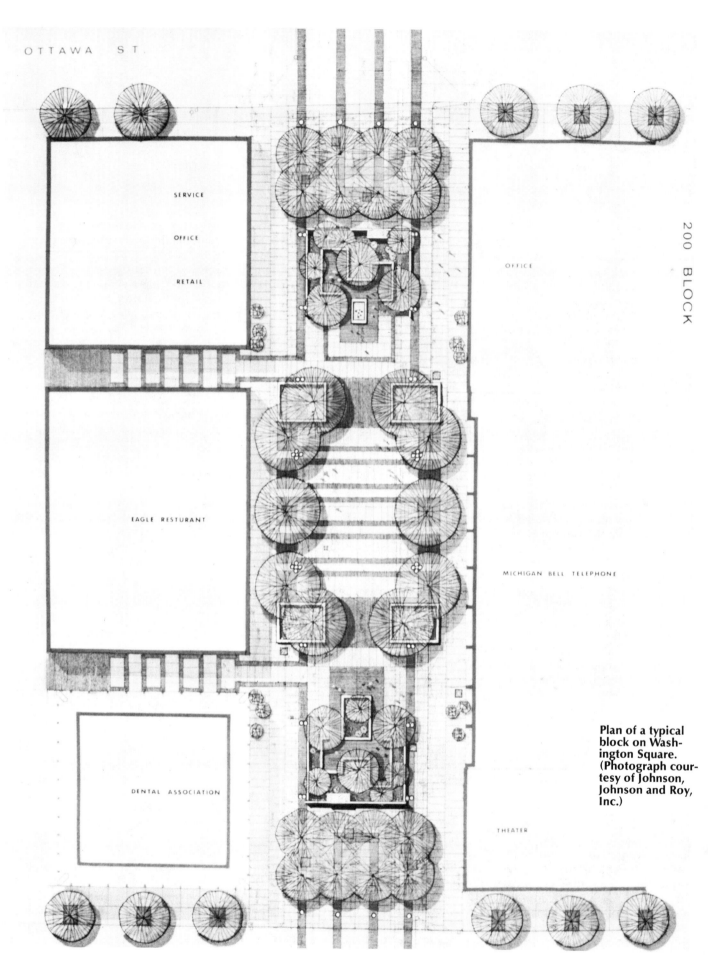

OTTAWA ST.

SERVICE

OFFICE

RETAIL

EAGLE RESTURANT

DENTAL ASSOCIATION

OFFICE

MICHIGAN BELL TELEPHONE

THEATER

Plan of a typical block on Washington Square. (Photograph courtesy of Johnson, Johnson and Roy, Inc.)

without obscuring views of other features. Smaller plants add color at different seasons of the year. Rhododendron, azaleas, pieris, bayberry, yews, ivy, and small trees such as the redbud and shadblow serviceberry are used.

NIGHT LIGHTING
Lighting is provided by dual luminaires on tall standards, and pedestrian scale lighting by twin opaque plexiglass cylinders. Clusters of the cylinders simulating large candelabras are used in the larger open areas of the square.

Accent lighting is provided by low indirect fixtures, softly illuminating low walls, sculpture, and planting.

In Retrospect

Washington Square is an important first phase in Lansing's downtown redevelopment. The mall provides a variety of activities and was expanded for three blocks to the north for pedestrian area on the Lansing Community College Campus. In addition, four semimall blocks were added to the south with widened sidewalk areas and some parking. Three of the blocks were accessed via one-way streets past parking booths. In 1990 two way traffic was permitted for a trial period on these three blocks with metered parking because some shoppers were frustrated with the network of one-way streets.

The mall and sidewalks in the downtown are maintained through a contract with a maintenance company administered through the Parks and Recreation Department.

The mall has greatly improved the physical appearance of the downtown and brought in new street activities. Property values have increased as has rental value. The mall is considered to be moderately successful.

Outdoor concession. (Photograph courtesy of Johnson, Johnson and Roy, Inc.)

Children's play
area. (Photograph
courtesy of Lansing
Park and Recrea-
tion Department.)

View of kiosk.
(Photograph cour-
tesy of Johnson,
Johnson and Roy,
Inc.)

View of brick and concrete paving and other street-scape treatment. (Photograph courtesy of Lansing Park and Recreation Department.)

Special events have room for people to gather on the mall. (Photograph courtesy of Lansing Park and Recreation Department.)

View of semimall (Parking Mall) area. (Photograph courtesy of Lansing Park and Recreation Department.)

Parkway Mall

Napa, California

Description

Parkway Mall is located in Napa, California, a city with 50,879 residents, located about 40 miles northeast of San Francisco. A three-block (1000-foot) length is a full mall with a large plaza area 120 × 120 feet.

Another portion is six blocks (2000 feet) long and is a semimall. The mall was developed to revitalize the downtown. The mall features new paving, lighting, fountains, a clock tower, sitting areas, children's play areas, and planting. The planners for the mall were Hall and Goodhue, and the

landscape architects were Sasaki Associates.

Two new department stores have also been built in the downtown, and new zoning was approved to rezone out all peripheral, competing commercial areas to comply with the General Plan for the City of Napa and Environs.

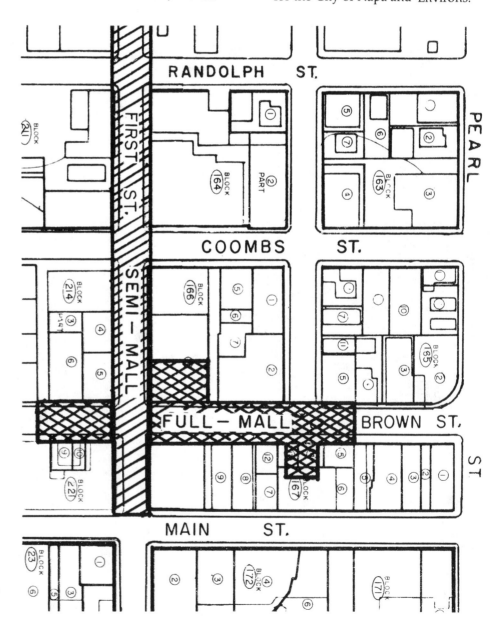

Location plan of mall.

The mall was funded by the Federal Neighborhood Development Program. The project was completed in August 1974, at a cost of $1.5 million for the full mall and $8 million for the semimall.

Development Strategy

Planning studies go back to the mid-1940s, when a preliminary study was done for urban redevelopment in the central business district (CBD). In 1952 a planning consultant prepared a master plan that was adopted by the City Council, but no action was taken regarding the CBD. In August 1959, an ad hoc group of citizens began a series of meetings to investigate urban renewal and gather information on methods of financing. Two years later, on August 30, 1961, this group of eight members was designated by the City Council as the Napa Urban Renewal Committee. The committee was enlarged to 28 members in May 1962, and recommendations were given to the City Council to establish a redevelopment agency and begin negotiations with the Federal Urban Renewal Agency in order to begin a renewal plan. In November 1962, the City Council created the Napa Community Redevelopment Agency. Not much happened, however, until June 1966, when a new planning director for the city was appointed.

The pace of action then began to pick up; a planning firm was retained, and by August 1968, the General Plan for the City of Napa and Environs was approved by the Planning Commission and adopted by the City Council in November. Also, in November 1968, "A Workable Pro-

View of mall showing clock tower, lighting, fountain, and paving. (Photographs courtesy of Sasaki Associates, Inc.)

gram for Community Improvement for Napa" received certification by HUD.

In January 1969, the City Council reactivated the Napa Community Redevelopment Agency, dormant since 1962. City council members became members of the agency, funds were applied for, and a public hearing was scheduled.

In December 1969, the redevelopment plan was adopted by the City Council. Funds were approved by HUD in January 1970, for the area called the Parkway Plaza Redevelopment. Construction got underway in 1971, with the reconstruction of one block on First Street from Coombs to Randolph. Three years later the entire mall was completed, along with two department stores and three off-street parking lots.

Design Features

The mall has many design features that have given the downtown a new vitality.

PAVING
The mall is paved predominantly in brick with concrete bands.

LIGHTING
Lights are clear round acrylic globes attached to wooden standards, to wooden trellis structures, and to a sculptural clock tower that acts as the focus of the large plaza area.

FOUNTAINS
A fountain is also part of the plaza area and provides a waterfall effect, with water flowing over natural stone into a pool.

PLANTING
Trees planted along the mall shade the sitting areas.

CHILDREN'S PLAY AREAS
These areas have wooden play equipment and sliding boards.

OVERHEAD STRUCTURES
A wooden trellis stretches throughout the full mall, providing shaded sitting areas and an interesting shadow pattern on the paving. Night lighting is incorporated into the structure.

OTHER STREET FURNISHINGS
These features include kiosks, bollards, raised planters, and other elements.

Night lighting effect.

In Retrospect

Napa has become one of the first small cities in California to reverse the trend toward suburban shopping centers and downtown decay, to the extent of building two new department stores in its downtown. This was partially accomplished by zoning policies that restrict major commercial development to downtown Napa's 324-acre Parkway Plaza Project for both the community and the county. Some commercial property on the periphery of the downtown has been downzoned to residential. This restrictive zoning works in Napa because the concept generally has citizen support.

During the past 5 years retail sales have not increased, but property values have risen. The mall has also acted as a catalyst for other development in the downtown. The main anchor store, Mervyn's, is very successful and is also closest to parking. A larger mall located adjacent to the Parkway Mall has overbuilt resulting in a negative for both malls with smaller shops being affected the most.

Parkway Mall is considered somewhat successful and has had some renovations since its original construction. The heavy trellises and vines used in front of the shops caused a shaded atmosphere, but was somewhat dark. This caused some tenants to move. The trellises have been removed and a more open atmosphere is being created. More nearby parking would also help the mall.

Sparks Street Mall

Ottawa, Ontario, Canada

Description

The Sparks Street Mall is located in Ottawa, Ontario, the Canadian capital, which has a population of 365,921. The mall forms a pedestrian area three blocks in length with a width of 60 feet.

At Elgin Street at the east end of Sparks Street, the mall connects with Confederation Square and is only one block from Parliament Hill to the north and a half block from the National Arts center along Elgin. The mall, which has been very successful, includes within its three blocks some of the most valuable properties in the city. More than $1 million in city taxes is collected in this area annually.

The mall features fountains, sculpture, kiosks, canopies, lighting, plant- ing, and sitting areas. The architects of the original mall were Helmer Associates. The recent renovations were designed by Cecelia Paine and Associates of Ottawa, and the SWA Group of Houston. The Sparks Street Mall was funded by the city and by assessment of property owners. It was completed in 1967 at a cost of $636,000. The mall renovation was carried out in the late 1980s.

Location map.

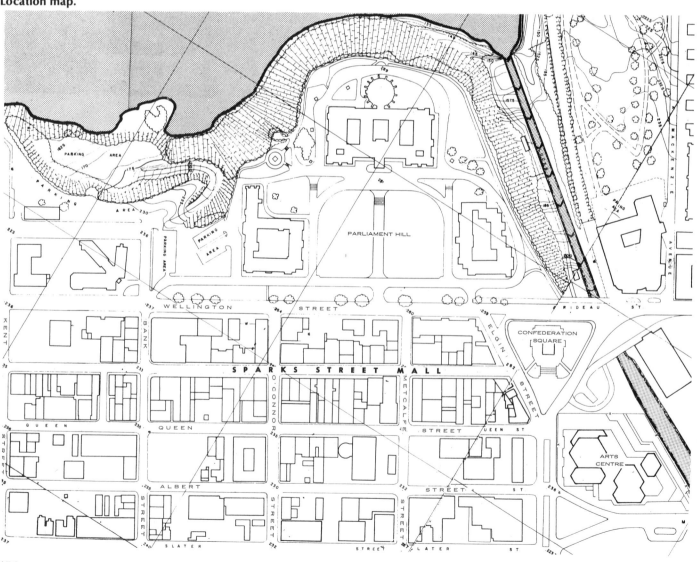

Development Strategy

In the late 1950s a well known town planner, Jacques Greber, suggested that Sparks Street might be a good location for a pedestrian mall. In September 1959, the Ottawa Board of Trade took businessmen, civic, and government officials to see a pedestrian precinct in Toledo, Ohio. Some of the businessmen were enthusiastic about the concept and formed the Sparks Street Development Association. The association wanted to create and test a mall on three blocks of Sparks Street. In early spring of 1960 the City Council agreed to approve necessary legislation and share the cost for a temporary mall up to a maximum of $15,000. The rest of the budget was to be raised by the merchant members of the Sparks Street Development Association. The mall was to open in May and be removed after Canada's Thanksgiving in October 1960.

A research committee studied traffic flow, parking, and retail sales during the duration of the mall experiment. The research data showed that the mall was a success, and in 1961 a second summer mall was funded by the merchants.

After a third temporary mall was built in 1962, it was decided that a permanent mall should be developed, and a citizens' committee was formed. A report was then presented to the Board of Control in October 1963.

City Hall was aware that the mall had the backing of the public and that deterioration of the downtown was about to lower tax revenues. The mall was therefore included in the 1965–1966 capital budget. The amount budgeted was $578,000, to be shared equally by the city and by owners abutting the mall. An amendment was inserted in enabling legislation so that the mall would proceed only if a majority of owners, representing one-half of the assessment involved, consented. In October 1965, Sparks Street owners offered to pay the cost to winterize another temporary mall, while the city provided snow removal. Consent was then obtained from more than 90 percent of the property owners, and approval to proceed was given by the Ontario Legislature in June, 1966.

A committee to provide for the welfare and maintenance of the mall

Entrance area at Sparks Street Mall. (Photographs by Ewald Richter.)

was also proposed. This committee would be composed of two members from the City Council, two Sparks Street property owners, and two merchants.

Design Features

FOUNTAINS
The mall features several fountains. The fountains have aerated jets of water that form focal areas in several locations in the granite streetscape pavement.

PAVING
The paving on the mall was redone with granite pavers.

SEATING
Benches that have backs are made of wood. Other seating is on sitting height walls and at outdoor eating areas.

NIGHT LIGHTING
Overhead wiring was placed underground on the original mall. The new lighting has cast iron poles with white globes in clusters.

PLANTERS
There are several different types of raised planters. Some are round and are planted with trees and flowers. Other planters are part of overhead canopies that have wire structures with vines growing on them to form feature elements.

OTHER ELEMENTS
Specially designed sculptural elements with lighting are located at the entrance to the mall. There are also canopies with planting, and other furnishings.

Fountain in granite paving area with raised seating area and canopy defining the space.

In Retrospect

The mall has the advantage of separating heavy pedestrian movement on Sparks Street from relatively unnecessary but congested vehicular circulation. The mall has improved rerouted bus traffic flow and stimulated business on Sparks Street.

Pedestrians like the mall; it is a recreational area for people and a very busy place. The taxes are the highest in the city, and no vacancies remain since the area became a mall.

Also, some problems anticipated from the change in traffic routes have not been as severe as many people predicted and have not adversely affected the general traffic flow through the center of Ottawa. The mall is now being expanded an additional block to link with the Garden of Provinces. Much new development has also taken place along the mall, including the Bank of Canada's new headquarters and several new office buildings.

The mall, built in the late 1960s, needed updating and was completely renovated in the late 1980s not only with a new design but with new utilities including sewer and electrical wiring for street lights. It also received a design award in 1988. Retail sales have increased somewhat along the mall due mostly to the large number of tourists. The mall also helped to generate other development in the downtown with the World Exchange Plaza one block south. The mall is used most at lunchtime, and property values have increased as has assessed rental value. Buildings along the mall are kept in good condition with 60 percent owned by the Federal Government. The Sparks Street Mall has been moderately successful.

Paving and lighting with clusters of globes.

Paving, lighting,
canopies, and
seating.

**Outdoor eating
areas and related
lighting in overhead
planters.**

**Eating area and
canopy elements
with vines growing
over wire structures.**

National Arts Center

The mall is less than half a block from the National Arts Center on Elgin Street. The Arts Center has three theatres to accommodate 3563 patrons, a dining lounge, an indoor–outdoor cafe, a bookstore, and a large underground public garage. The National Arts Center is also adjacent to the Rideau Canal, which connects Ottawa with Kingston and the St. Lawrence River. The canal is 123.5 miles long, with 47 locks and 24 dams. Near the Arts Center the canal has a very urban character and with its pedestrian walks provides, in effect, an extension of the recreational activity provided by the mall.

Sitting area with wood benches on iron frame and raised tree planters forming a bosque.

Penn Square

Reading, Pennsylvania

Description

Penn Square is located in Reading, Pennsylvania, a city with 78,686 residents, 60 miles northwest of Philadelphia. It is a pedestrian-oriented square in the 500 block of Penn Street that has been closed to through traffic. The 400 block has also been renovated and allows two lanes of traffic in each direction with drop-off areas for buses, taxis, and deliveries.

On the northeast end of the 500 block there is a convenience parking area for 18 cars and access to a service lane. The service lane is unique to this plan and allows deliveries to stores with no other access. Each block is about 530 feet long and 160 feet wide. The square features two cascading fountains, sitting areas, brick and concrete paving patterns,

night lighting, extensive landscaping, and two sheltered bus stops on the 400 block. Landscape architects for the mall were The Delta Group. The square was developed with funds from a variety of sources, including the Pennsylvania Department of Community Affairs, the city of Reading, Berks County, donations from local merchants, and a special tax assessment on Penn Square property owners. The Penn Square project was completed in May, 1975, at a cost of $1.6 million.

Development Strategy

In 1969 local businessmen, with the support of the Chamber of Commerce and city government, began to look for possible improvements in downtown Reading. The Downtown

Core Revitalization Committee of the Chamber of Commerce, working with an architect, proposed preliminary plans that were presented to the City Council.

In 1971 the mayor appointed the Mayor's Committee of 25 to spearhead the Penn Square Project. The committee worked with the Reading Redevelopment Authority, which was founded in 1952. This group was able to secure financial assistance as follows: the Pennsylvania Department of Community Affairs, $758,000; the city of Reading, $450,000; Berks County, $175,000; donations from local merchants, $90,000; and property owners in Penn Square, $180,000 in the form of a special tax assessment. In 1972 an architectural firm was retained to carry out planning and design studies for the square. In August 1973, construction

Plan of Penn Square.

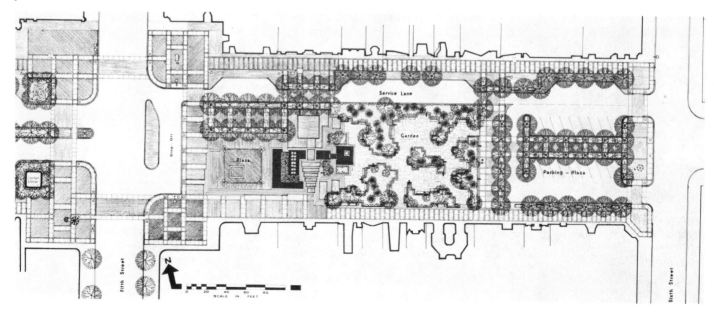

began. The City Council has established a seven-member Penn Square Commission to oversee the management of programs, promotions, and activities.

Building facades are also being restored, and signs and graphics controlled.

Design Features

The square has attracted shoppers, strollers, and office workers who bring their lunches to eat on benches and steps.

FOUNTAINS

Two types of cascading fountains are located on the square. One is bowl shaped with water pouring from it, while the other fountain has 12 jets. The fountains have a capacity of 8000 gallons per minute, provided by three pumps.

GARDEN AREA

Located toward the center of the plaza, a garden provides a quiet area offering many benches on which to relax. The garden is paved in flagstone and consists of a series of several spaces defined by plant beds.

PAVING

Paving is in a brick and concrete pattern. The brick is red and reflects the architectural heritage of Reading. The concrete bands add rhythm and interest.

PLANTING

There are 239 trees on the square. Deciduous trees such as oak, linden, and plane trees are used, along with evergreens, for example, hemlock, pine, and spruce. There are also shrubs such as rhododendron and azalea, as well as ground cover and bulbs.

NIGHT LIGHTING

As part of the development, new street lights, low level bollard lights, walkway plaza lights, and landscape area lights have been used. The mercury vapor type was chosen.

FACILITIES FOR THE DISABLED

All public facilities are accessible to the disabled. At each intersection, ramps have been provided in the pav-

View of fountain, which is a major feature of this urban square.

Cascading effect of water.

ing system for the convenience of persons in wheelchairs.

PUBLIC STRUCTURES

Two sheltered bus stops in the 400 block of Penn Street are provided, and a comfort station is planned in the future. A newsstand that also sells lottery tickets is located near Sixth Street.

In Retrospect

Penn Square forms an interesting framework in which a variety of activities take place. Throughout construction of the project most merchants maintained their former sales level or had increased sales. During construction there was a positive marketing approach with special events such as Lucky Sales Days.

The mall is busiest at lunchtime, and is a gathering place in the downtown during months with mild temperatures. It also is used for downtown festivals. The mall is considered not successful by many, but not all observers. Over the past 5 years retail sales have not increased and the mall does not appear to be generating other retail development on adjacent blocks. Several buildings are vacant, and are not being well maintained. Some merchants would prefer to have the block open to traffic, but the mall provides the major urban space that is centrally located in the downtown. The space provides a sense of place for the downtown and has amenities such as the fountain, brick and concrete paving, seating, and night lighting. It has also received design recognition. At present the mall appears to need some updating of design and some renovation.

Aerated jets of water provide a focus for the fountain, which is lighted for night effect.

Brick and concrete paving pattern provides rhythm in its design. Bollards with built-in lights and tree grates are also part of the design.

Semimalls

Hamilton Mall

Allentown, Pennsylvania

Description

Hamilton Mall is located in Allentown, Pennsylvania, a city of 103,758 people, about 55 miles north of Philadelphia. Hamilton Street, the major downtown shopping street, has been turned into a semimall four blocks in length. Hamilton Street previously had five lanes of traffic, but has been narrowed to a roadway width of 22 feet. Automobiles, buses, and taxicabs can use this semimall. The semimall was developed to preserve and revitalize the central business district. The architects, engineers, and landscape architects for the mall were Cope, Linder, and Walmsley.

Hamilton Mall features an extensive cantilevered canopy system on both sides of the street, stretching the length of the mall and unifying its design. The mall also features new paving, lighting, traffic signalization, fountains, planting, kiosks, sitting areas, and heated bus stops. Within easy walking distance of the mall are 7500 parking spaces. Activities on the mall include fashion shows, arts and crafts festivals, sidewalk sales, and Pennsylvania Dutch Day.

The semimall was funded by the Pennsylvania Department of Community Affairs and the city of Allentown. Construction was completed in November 1973, at a cost of $5 million.

Development Strategy

In the mid-1960s the downtown was beginning to show signs of deterioration, with falling receipts and a dwindling tax base. Local merchants and public officials decided that a major study of the entire central city area should be made.

In April 1967, a planning firm was retained to begin the center city study. The Progressive Center City Allentown Organization paid $15,000 toward the first study. Represented in the group were merchants, financial institutions, utilities, and private corporations. The city and state also helped fund the study, which reviewed such areas as traffic flow, markets, and treatment of residential areas in the center city.

The study, which was completed in February 1969, recommended that a mall be developed on Hamilton Street and that residential areas surrounding the downtown be rehabilitated.

Design work on the mall began, and in February 1972, construction started. The mall was to be completed by the Christmas season of 1973.

The Pennsylvania Department of Community Affairs provided $2.5

Plan of mall.

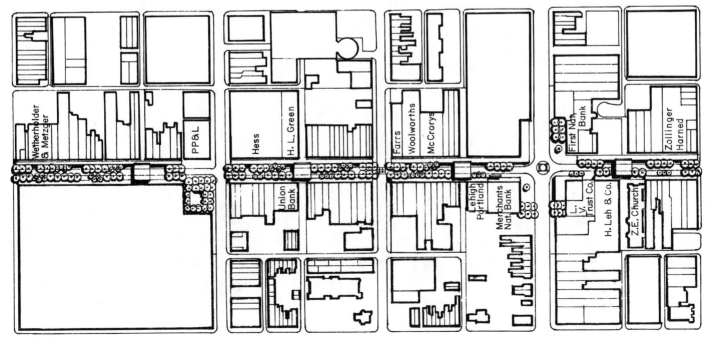

million of the funding, with the city of Allentown matching this with $2.5 million of general obligation bonds, for a total of $5 million. The Allentown Redevelopment Authority coordinated the overall planning for the project.

Design Features

CANOPIES

The canopy system unifies the entire mall. There are 4800 linear feet of steel and Plexiglas in the cantilevered canopies. They provide some weather protection and have heating elements in gutters and downspouts to melt snow and ice. The canopy system is 14 feet high along walks and 12.5 feet wide. A 1-foot transition space between the canopy and existing buildings causes some problems at

Canopy covering brick sidewalk.

entrances to buildings in rainy weather. The canopy continues across intersections and increases in height above the street.

LIGHTING
Lighting is incorporated in the canopy system: 3000 incandescent lamps in round lexan globes line both the inside and the outside of the structure. Additional lighting is used at midblock, where metal halide lamps on high poles emit a brighter and more efficient light on the scene below. Along both sides of the roadway, 240 bollards 3 feet high with built-in lighting also help illuminate the area used by vehicles.

PAVING
Hamilton Street originally had 12-foot-wide sidewalks. These have been widened to 29 feet and are paved with brick and concrete. The roadway through the mall has bituminous paving, but there is a concrete surface on drop-off areas, which are used for passenger and merchandise pickup.

RAISED PLANTERS
Sixty planters made of concrete are used on the mall for trees, shrubs, and flowers.

View of streetscape with bollards and sidewalk areas.

View of canopy areas across width of street.

PLANTING

The mall has 130 trees, many of them red oaks planted directly in the walk areas with tree grates used around them. The trees and grates are integrated into the paving design. Other planting includes shrubs, ground cover, and flowers.

FOUNTAINS

The mall also features several fountains with aerated jets of water. Some of these are surrounded by low concrete walls similar to the planters.

OTHER FURNISHINGS

Kiosks are also part of the street furnishings. They are surfaced with porcelain enamel to limit graffiti. Sitting areas, heated bus stops, and traffic signals have also been designed for the mall. In addition, new utility lines have been placed beneath the center of the roadway as part of the mall construction, to limit disturbance to the mall in the future.

In Retrospect

Hamilton Mall was developed to provide a safe, attractive, easily accessible shopping area. The original idea of a full mall was abandoned when a test period that was to last for 90 days was stopped after 1 week because of complaints from merchants.

In the 1970s the mall spurred investment of over $30 million in new buildings, additions, and parking structures. The tax base increased as did sales. In the past 5 years retail sales have not increased. The semi-mall with its streetscape has been adequately maintained and gets its greatest use from pedestrians at lunchtime.

The mall is considered somewhat successful, is noted for its design, which provides an image for the downtown, and is used widely by the entire Allentown community.

View of paving, planters, and bollard lights.

Captain's Walk

New London, Connecticut

Description

Captain's Walk is located on State Street in New London, Connecticut, the core city within the southeastern Connecticut region. Although New London has a population of only 29,000, it serves a region of 225,000 people.

A semimall was originally chosen to meet the need for a physical plan that could be produced at a cost in scale with the downtown economy. The mall was six blocks in length, with one-way traffic on the lower portion between O'Neill Drive and Water Street. The upper blocks have two-way traffic between Huntington and Washington Streets. However, traffic was prohibited from the central two and one-half block portion of the mall, which was oriented toward pedestrians and had only emergency and service vehicle access on a 12-foot-wide curvilinear path. The mall featured a nautical theme that reflected the past history of New London as a seaport, whaling town, and sailors' port-of-call. Traffic was reintroduced to the two and one-half blocks, which was a full mall in 1991. The new streetscape features pavers in a herringbone pattern. The original mall was designed by landscape architects Johnson and Dee. The mall

renovation was designed by the Maguire Group Inc. Captain's Walk was developed initially with funds from the Downtown New London Association, the Federal Urban Renewal Agency, and the state. The project was completed in November 1973, at a cost of $1.5 million. The new renovation was completed in 1991 at a cost of $1 million.

Development Strategy

A pedestrian mall concept was exhibited in early 1969. This design included pedestrian and vehicular circulation systems, parking locations, service access, staging, and environ-

View of original mall showing paving, canopies, and other features. The canopies appeared as abstract sails and the mounded grass islands were nicknamed "whales."

mental improvements. The proposal became part of the Winthrop Urban Renewal Project. A full mall concept for the six blocks was abandoned in 1971 because of uncertainties about federal funding and inability to resolve legal and service problems.

The combination semimall on three and one-half blocks and full mall on two and one-half blocks was then selected as the scheme most appropriate to the physical setting. The objective of the design was to create a new setting that would provide visual excitement and a new identity for the downtown. Also, State Street had high quality shops and professional, banking, and financial

services for the region, which the mall would complement and strengthen. The Downtown New London Association raised $50,000 in voluntary funds, based on a benefit assessment formula, as seed money to get the project started. Once this commitment had been obtained, the City Council endorsed the project and formal applications were made. Funding was provided by the Federal Urban Renewal Agency and by the state. In addition to the semimall, in November 1970 the Governor Winthrop parking garage was opened. It provides 406 parking spaces and features a covered pedestrian bridge that links directly to Captain's Walk. Another

205 municipal parking spaces were upgraded in 1973, and groundbreaking took place for a 550-car garage in the lower Captain's Walk area.

The planning process began again in 1988 when the full mall, which was not an economic success, had increasing competition from the Crystal Mall, which opened in 1985 in neighboring Waterford. A coalition of city agencies, downtown property owners, developers, and the public was involved in the decision.

Traffic was introduced to the two and one-half block full mall area of the original project in 1991.

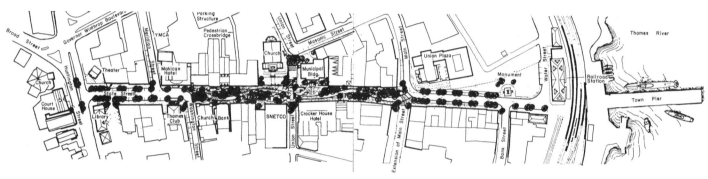

Plan of original mall.

View of new streetscape while under construction.

Design Features

PAVING

Granite curbs and red pavers in a herringbone pattern are used for sidewalk areas. The sidewalk width is minimal and does not allow for seating areas.

PLANTING

The block between Washington and Huntington has existing street trees in islands adjacent to the sidewalk areas. These islands have granite curbs and separate some of the parallel parking spaces. The other blocks have new sidewalks but lack street trees.

NIGHT LIGHTING

Street lighting, while the project was under construction, was from the original fixtures, which are 35 feet high, with clear globes and 100-watt deluxe white mercury bulbs.

OTHER FURNISHINGS

These furnishings include cast iron bollards painted black. These bollards are featured adjacent to handicap ramps at street intersections and at some major buildings along the street. An existing clock is also part of the street furnishings.

In Retrospect

The original six block mall with two and one-half blocks closed to traffic was not an economic success. Although the full mall area created a relaxed environment with a feeling of congenial ambience, it lacked adequate vitality and did not encourage shoppers to spend money downtown. In addition, a new shopping mall, Crystal Mall, opened in 1985 in Waterford, further siphoning off potential customers.

As the suburbs grew New London also ceased to be the retail hub of eastern Connecticut.

Although vacancy rates have varied from less than 30 to over 50 percent, the entire picture is not bleak. Some of the restaurants, cafes, office supply stores, and established retailers are doing well, and developers are renovating important buildings such as the Lena Building next to City Hall, on Captain's Walk.

More than 1.5 million people pass through New London each year on their way to Long Island Sound, Mystic, and Groton. The reopening of Captain's Walk is the first in a four phase program for downtown improvements. A planned multimillion dollar maritime heritage park and visitor center will also help give the city an improved image.

Wyoming Avenue Plaza

Scranton, Pennsylvania

Description

Wyoming Avenue Plaza is located in the 100 Block of Wyoming Avenue in downtown Scranton, Pennsylvania, a city of 88,117 residents. The mall was planned to facilitate pedestrian use along Wyoming Avenue where the two major department stores in the downtown were located. The mall is 650 feet in length and has a general width of 100 feet between opposite building facades.

Wyoming Avenue, which is a two-way street, had four lanes of traffic and two parking lanes. In the final semimall concept, on-street parking is removed and the street narrowed from 62 to 40 feet. This allows for much wider pedestrian walk areas and related amenities. Bus pull-off areas are also provided to facilitate transit use.

The mall has a clock tower, sculpture, children's play area, interlocking concrete and precast concrete pavers, and pedestrian walk lighting as well as street lighting with utility wires

placed underground. Raised planters, seating, kiosks, new traffic poles, drinking fountains, flower pots, bollards, and much new planting are also provided. Architects, engineers, planners, and landscape architects for the mall were Bellante, Clauss, Miller and Nolan. The mall was funded by Community Development Program, Economic Development Administration funds, and private funds from the merchants in the 100 Block of Wyoming Avenue. The mall was completed in 1979, at a construction cost of $862 thousand. Construction began on the project in May 1978, after some delay due to an extension to the project being considered.

Development Strategy

The primary purpose of the mall was to begin the revitalization of downtown Scranton, with the 100 Block of Wyoming as the first step in the process. This block was the most important single one in the Central Business District, accounting for

about 60 percent of the tax base of the city. Two large department stores are located here along with several banks, a variety of shops, restaurants, and some offices.

Many plans and traffic studies had been done in the 1960s but little had been accomplished in the downtown until 1974, when some of the merchants on the 100 Block became interested in the idea of a mall. A design firm was contacted to develop feasibility studies on locating the mall in this block and alternate concepts for full and transit or semimalls. These plans were exhibited during a week when the 100 Block was closed to traffic during Downtown Shopping Days. Interest in the idea of a mall was generated, but controversy developed over what type of mall should be built, if the 100 Block was the place to begin, and if one block was enough for the first phase. During this period, funds from the Community Development Program were available but were not adequate to build a design having a canopy sys-

Plan of semimall.

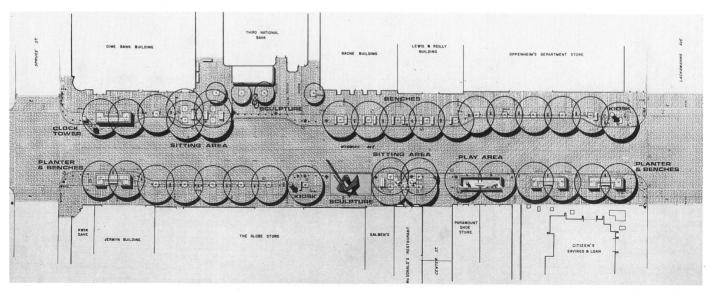

tem. The merchants decided on a mall without the canopy and on a two-lane curvilinear design that would allow buses on the mall during shopping hours and both cars and buses on the mall at all other times.

The merchants also agreed to assess themselves for $100,000 to show the city they were willing to contribute money toward the block on which they were located. The city then agreed to using $300,000 of Community Development Funds for the mall.

City Council approved the idea of the mall and passed an ordinance so that the street could be narrowed. This was approved on November 24, 1976.

An interesting event then occurred. To develop the mall properly, $1 million was needed. It became possible in 1977 to apply to the Economic Development Administration for the remaining funds needed. In order to accomplish this, the City Council had to approve the application for funding. On the first vote, March 23, 1977, City Council, by a 3 to 2 vote, vetoed

the application because they were not convinced a mall was an answer to the city's needs for revitalization.

The merchants, news media, and public became very outspoken about the need for the mall as the first step in revitalizing the downtown, and after many newspaper and television editorials, and work by the merchants, Chamber of Commerce, the Mayor, and others, another Council meeting was held on discussion of the application for funding. The application for EDA funds was approved by a 3 to 2 vote on April 6, 1977.

After the project had been funded in August 1977, and during development of final construction drawings, the major property owner on the 100 Block of Wyoming Avenue publicly objected to the two-lane scheme originally agreed upon, claiming there would be traffic problems. That claim was never substantiated, but wishing the revitalization of the block to move forward, the Mayor proposed a compromise solution to the merchants. This semimall removed the parking

lanes and narrowed the street to 40 feet. It will be possible to narrow the street further to create a two-lane scheme or a full mall in the future.

Although the majority of the merchants backed the two-lane plan, all agreed that for the project to proceed on schedule and to receive funding and eliminate possible lawsuits, the Mayor's proposal was the only feasible alternative. The project proceeded on this basis and approval from all parties was obtained.

Design Features

The mall has many design features that create an interesting environment in which to shop, stroll, eat lunch, and have special events.

PAVING
The entire base plane of the mall is paved with concrete pavers. Walk areas are in a rustic colored concrete brick paver with aggregate concrete bands to give rhythm to the design. The roadway has granite curbs and is

View of mall adjacent to raised planter areas.

View of streetscape treatment with interlocking concrete z-pavers, lighting, and sitting areas.

View of drop-off areas adjacent to bank with granite bollards defining the area.

paved with a thicker concrete brick paver.

The installation of interlocking concrete pavers and aggregate concrete pavers used for bands gives color, texture, and rhythm to the mall's paving design. Three-foot high granite bollards provide interest and additional safety at bus drop-off areas.

SCULPTURE

Two sculptures are proposed on the mall to act as feature elements and to provide cultural amenities in the downtown.

CLOCK TOWER

A clock tower is provided near the intersection of Wyoming Avenue and Spruce Street. The clock has lighted faces that are for night time viewing.

KIOSKS

Two kiosks are located on the mall. Both are of kynar treated bronze aluminum and have night lighting. One serves as a directory while the other encloses electrical equipment.

PLAY AREA

A small children's play area, provided with wood play equipment, is included so that all age groups can enjoy the mall.

INTERSECTION SIGNALIZATION

Contemporary traffic signal structures enhance the intersections at Spruce Street and Lackawanna Avenue. These have a bronze color and incorporate pedestrian walk signals and police call boxes.

NIGHT LIGHTING

Lighting is provided on 30-foot duranodic bronze aluminum poles for the roadway and on 12-foot high duranodic poles for pedestrian areas. Up-lights are used to illuminate the sculptures and trees in raised planters.

SEATING

Redwood benches with backs are provided facing in two directions for views along the mall as well as singly in other sitting areas. Seating is also incorporated in raised concrete planters. Granite tables are available for eating or playing cards.

PLANTING

Shade trees are used to form a canopy along both sides of the mall. London Plane trees were selected for their hardiness and interesting bark and are planted in both sidewalk areas and in raised planters. Evergreen shrubs are also planted in the raised planters as well as in some granite pots.

In Retrospect

The Wyoming Avenue Plaza has acted as a catalyst for downtown revitalization. It has sparked an interest in the downtown and inspired those interested in improving it to work together. It also created a sense of place for the downtown.

During this period of planning for the mall, a commission on architecture and urban design was approved by the Mayor and City Council at the request of an Ad Hoc Committee to help improve the aesthetics of the city and to encourage the use of up to 1 percent of funds for works of art on public projects. Wyoming Avenue Plaza is considered moderately successful.

In 1983 three additional semimall blocks were completed based on the success of the original block as the initial phase for the renovation of the overall streetscape of the downtown. One block was the 200 block of Wyoming Avenue and the other blocks were the 300 and 400 blocks of Lackawanna Avenue adjacent to the original semimall. The three new blocks were funded by Federal Highway Administration Funds through the Pennsylvania Department of Transportation. The three blocks feature brick and concrete sidewalks with wider pedestrian areas, and similar types of street furnishings used on the 100 block of Wyoming Avenue to provide continuity to the streetscape design. In addition, three other blocks in the downtown were planned for renovation in the next phase of downtown revitalization, and design for these blocks was taken into the construction drawings.

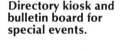

Directory kiosk and bulletin board for special events.

Harbor Centre

Sheboygan, Wisconsin

Description

Harbor Centre (formerly called Plaza 8), began as a full mall, located on 8th Street in Sheboygan, Wisconsin, a city with a population of 48,085. The full mall, three and one-half blocks in length, stretched from Ontario Avenue south past New York Avenue. It was 1500 feet in length with a right-of-way of 80 feet, and widened to form a large public plaza adjacent to the library.

The purpose of the mall was to revitalize the downtown shopping area. Pedestrian and vehicular traffic were separated, and convenient parking space was provided. The original mall had Barton Ashman Associates as planners and Lawrence Halprin and Associates as the landscape architects.

Design features of the mall included a fountain with a cascading effect, new paving, lighting, planting, sitting areas, and other furnishings. The mall was funded by the Federal Urban Renewal Agency and by the city. The project was completed in July 1976, at a cost of $1.6 million. The mall was recently renovated in 1990–1991 and traffic was reintroduced to the blocks.

Development Strategy

Downtown Sheboygan has experienced great pressures for change. There was a gradual deterioration of existing facilities and services, along with declining property and taxable values. The overall objective of the mall is to return the downtown to a sound condition physically, functionally, and economically.

The Sheboygan Redevelopment Authority is the official agency responsible for the redevelopment of the downtown. The authority was created by the Common Council in 1966 and consists of seven appointed,

unpaid commissioners, two aldermen, and five citizens. A master plan developed in 1966 for the rebuilding of the downtown proposed a pedestrian plaza and the filing of an application for a Federal Urban Renewal Agency grant. In 1967 a large regional shopping center opened on the periphery of Sheboygan. This generated action by the city and the Chamber of Commerce, in a 50–50 financial partnership as they moved ahead into formal renewal planning. When the application reached HUD, the agency was impressed by the city's initiative and funded the first phase of the project.

The mall was submitted and approved by the Common Council in January 1972. The federal government approved the project in July 1972.

The project was funded for 75 percent of its $1.6 million cost by the Federal Urban Renewal Agency and for the remaining 25 percent by the city. The city's share will be paid through its provision of the new library and new parking facilities. The design was developed to maintain and strengthen Sheboygan's competitive position as a regional and metropolitan shopping center. Functional, economic, and aesthetic values were introduced to complement modernized retailing methods.

The full mall was also developed to reduce vehicular and pedestrian conflicts in the downtown shopping area. Short-term parking for shoppers is provided. This is convenient for those using the mall.

Design Features

PAVING

The paving on the mall is concrete with a 2-foot wide band of pavers along curb areas. Pavers are also used in the 4 × 6 foot tree pit areas.

SEATING

Benches are used which are made of rod iron and mahogany.

LIGHTING

Cast aluminum poles and fixtures in turn of the century design are used.

PLANTING

Little-leaf lindens and honeylocust trees are used in the streetscape design.

As an additional feature at the southern end of the mall, a new municipal library was constructed and set back 50 feet to form a large planted space. The space is mounded 3 to 4 feet and planted with ash, oak, and birch trees to form a small forest in the downtown.

FOUNTAIN

An interesting water feature is located in the space adjacent to the library. The fountain is formed of concrete elements with water bubbling out of concrete blocks and then cascading down a series of lower blocks to echo one of the Indian definitions of the name "Sheboygan," originally meaning "place of rumbling waters." The fountain's waterfall has a drop of approximately 10 feet with a flow of 10,000 gallons per minute.

In Retrospect

The plaza represented one of the last large projects financed by the Federal Urban Renewal Agency.

The full mall was considered not successful. The mall did not help the economy of the downtown as expected, and retail sales have not improved over the past 5 years. Also, the mall did not help to generate additional retail development on adjacent blocks, and property values did not increase. Some people felt the

View of the original mall before it was renovated with the street reopened to traffic. (Photographs courtesy of the Sheboygan Department of City Development.)

View of streetscape with brick pavers along curb.

design of the mall was inappropriate for the area.

Over time it was decided to renovate the original blocks allowing traffic back on the streets for more activity. The blocks were re-constructed as a streetscape in 1990–1991.

View of streetscape with new lights and benches.

View of plaza adjacent to the mall in front of the library.

Broadway Plaza

Tacoma, Washington

Description

Broadway Plaza began as a full mall located in downtown Tacoma, Washington, a city with a population of 164,000 people, 25 miles south of Seattle. The mall was developed to revitalize the downtown and create a pedestrian precinct. Broadway Plaza extends for two double blocks (1380 feet) and is 80 feet wide. Two blocks

were originally a full mall with two semimall blocks added in 1977. Design features included large covered areas that served as bus stops and rest areas, as well as fountains, pools, performing and display stages, two children's play areas, lighting, and planting. The original mall was designed by architects Harris, and Reed and Litzenberger and James McGranahan. The first phase of the

Relationship of central business district to original mall. (Photographs courtesy of Tacoma Community Development Department.)

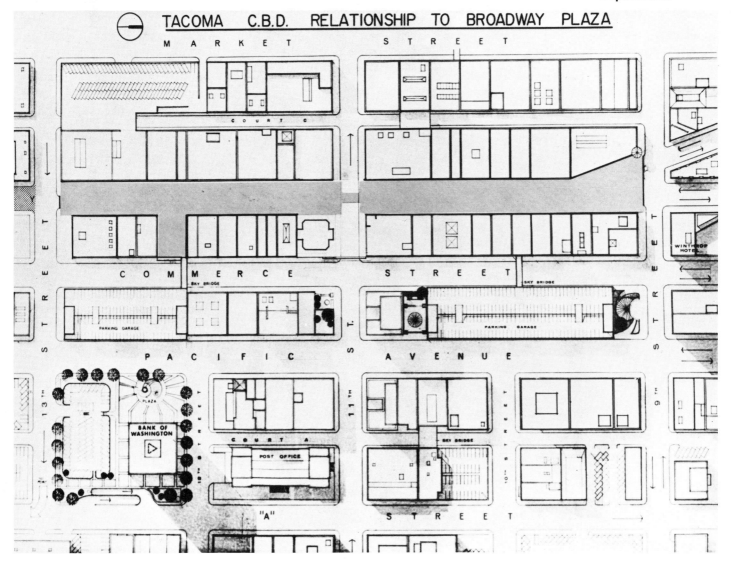

TACOMA C.B.D. RELATIONSHIP TO BROADWAY PLAZA

mall was financed by Federal Urban Renewal Agency funds, including noncash city matching funds. The mall was completed in May 1974, at a cost of $1.5 million, the extension being funded by an Economic Development Administration grant.

In the mid-1980s automobile traffic was permitted on one block. Two years later the second block was opened to through traffic. Both blocks have one lane in each direction and limited on-street parking. In effect the full mall has been renovated into a semimall with its related streetscape.

Development Strategy

The plaza was proposed in 1944, but serious planning did not begin until the mid-1960s.

A team management approach was utilized in the planning, design, and implementation of the Broadway Plaza. A unique partnership between the private and public sectors evolved, from which came not only the plaza but also two parking structures built with little cost to the city. A gift of $4 million worth of garages to the city by the private sector

generated over $13 million in federal grants.

A team of representatives from all city departments, private utilities, private businesses, and public officials was established. The team's first objective was to select a design concept and define program requirements. An architectural team of two firms on a joint venture basis was selected.

Public hearings were held that gave citizens a chance to review plans and offer opinions. A storefront office was also manned for two Saturdays to talk with people about the design and to

Photograph of street before the mall was developed looking from 9th Street south.

listen to suggestions. On two occasions the city closed the street to all traffic to test the impact on the surrounding area.

Program development also required conformance with a detailed state law on pedestrian malls. Numerous legal requirements had to be met and resolved, as Broadway Plaza was the first pedestrian mall to be built in the state.

When the full pedestrian mall was not a success economically it was renovated in the mid-1980s with traffic and limited parking reintroduced.

Design Features

PAVING
The sidewalk areas are paved with aggregate concrete and red brick pavers placed in bands. A few larger areas of brick are also used for some cross walks.

LIGHTING
Night lighting is provided by clusters of clear, round acrylic globes on metal standards.

SEATING
Wood benches with backs and arm rests are located on the mall. A seating height coping is also used around the fountain, which is a feature element.

PLANTING
Street trees and annuals are placed in low planters as a major element of the streetscape treatment. The planters have wrought iron railings around them.

View of original full mall and logo.

View north from 9th of semimall and municipal building.

View of streetscape with fenced planter.

OTHER FEATURES

A fountain made of concrete elements that has waterfalls and pools is a feature of the streetscape. This fountain was part of the original mall design. There is also a clock located at Le Roy Jewelers.

In Retrospect

Initially sales increased along the full mall, and a double block semimall was completed in 1977. The mall had special events such as auto and boat shows, bake sales, art shows, and music festivals. Over a period of time, however, the anchor department store left. Apparently, better timing was needed, for the mall was completed too late to compete with the opening of a large outlying retail shopping center and the entire downtown was hurt economically.

The original mall and now semimall did help to generate new development, and financial services business along with retail shops are located on the mall. Also, a Cornerstone Development Project in addition to others have recently boosted the downtown.

The introduction of traffic on the two blocks seems to be a positive step. The original 80 foot right-of-way may have been too large to close to traffic. There is more vitality now with an increase of pedestrian traffic on the street and less vacancy; the area has begun to turn around with the semimall considered a success.

View of fountain with waterfalls.

Transit Malls

16th Street Mall

Denver, Colorado

Description

Denver's 16th Street Mall is a 13-block long transit mall that opened in October 1982. The mall has an 80-foot right-of-way with a 22-foot tree-lined pedestrian promenade down the center for the middle six blocks with a 10-foot lane on each side for specially designed shuttle buses. At the mall's end blocks, the pedestrian area and transitway join and the trees shift to one side to facilitate shuttle areas. The mall has granite paving, precast tree pits with honeylocust trees, custom lighting, and other street furnishings. All nonemergency vehicles are excluded from the mall except at cross-streets. The shuttle bus system has free fares and carries passengers along the mall at 70-second intervals during peak periods and 3.5-minute intervals the rest of the time.

The transit mall was accomplished with 80 percent funding from the Urban Mass Transportation Administration and the remainder from the Regional Transportation District. The overall cost of the project totalled $76.1 million with $29.5 million for mall construction, $5.1 million for an initial fleet of shuttle buses, and the remainder for two transfer stations and renovation of the RTD administration building. The mall was designed by I.M. Pei and Partners, Architects and Hanna/Olin, Ltd. Landscape Architects.

Development Strategy

Denver's 16th Street has been the City's major retail shopping corridor since the 1890s. Beginning in the 1960s there was increased competition from suburban shopping centers along with some deteriorating storefronts and a number of dead spots on 16th Street.

In 1971, the board of directors of Downtown Denver, Inc. (DDI) a business advocacy group announced that it favored a mall concept. Several proposals were studied over the next 4 years, but no funding was available. At the same time the Regional Transportation District (RTD) was reviewing methods to alleviate congestion of buses in the downtown.

View of transit mall. (Photograph courtesy of The Denver Partnership.)

View of granite
paving, lighting,
and banners.

View of streetscape
with transit lane,
lighting, and plant-
ing. Specially de-
signed tree pits
were used so trees
would have uniform
growth.

187

The RTD and DDI began jointly exploring ways to improve both groups objectives, and in 1976 plans for a mall were revived with assistance from the city. In 1977, I.M. Pei and Partners developed a model of the 13-block transit mall with transfer stations at each end. The plan received support of most businesses and construction began in February 1980 for the $29 million dollar mall.

The Mall Management District

In 1978 business leaders initiated an amendment to Denver's City Charter creating a special mall benefit district to pay for the maintenance, management, and operation of the mall. The original district included properties between 15th and 17th streets, but in 1984 was expanded to cover about 865 property owners within a 70-block area of the downtown. The day-to-day management of the mall is directed by the staff of the Denver Partnership under a management contract with the mall's district board. The mall's shuttle bus service and transfer stations are operated by the RFD.

Mixed-use zoning, which was introduced to control the physical development along the mall, received approval in December 1981. It provides design guidelines on new buildings within 125 feet of either side of the 80-foot mall right-of-way and encouraged a mixed-use development and streetscape amenities. The new zoning also sets requirements, incentives, and space premiums for developers and owners who provide amenities such as plazas, skylight exposures, etc. The zoning also raises potential densities and sets alternatives to high-rise office structures.

Design Features

PAVING
The transit mall is paved in an indigenous native indian type of pattern in red and gray granite slabs.

PLANTING
The 22-foot promenade down the center of the mall is planted with honeylocust trees. Oaks are also used on the mall. The trees are planted in a vault type of system that has four precast concrete panels and a perforated lid about 10 × 10 feet that allows air to circulate over the soil mix. Granite pavers are placed over the lid, which has a cast iron grate with adjustable cut out rings for the trees' development. Rectangular openings in the planter walls allow feeder roots to grow into surrounding soil. The vaults have an open bottom where drain pipes can be placed. This system also limits compaction of the soil in the vault.

LIGHTING
Special lighting was designed for the mall; however, the luminaires are closely spaced and perhaps too imposing.

SEATING
Wood benches provide comfortable seating for the mall.

OTHER FURNISHINGS
There are also planter pots, telephone kiosks, signage, vendor's kiosks, fountains, and outdoor eating areas.

In Retrospect

The transitway has been successful in several ways. Ridership on the mall's 26 shuttle buses averages 40,000 per workday, and with the transfer station have relieved downtown traffic congestion.

The mall has helped to generate economic development and restoration throughout the downtown and was the catalyst for the Tabor Center development (280,000 square foot new retail), which contains a 420-room hotel, 120,000 square foot of retail, a 1900-car parking garage, and two office towers totaling 1.2 million square feet. Local business leaders also credit the mall as a catalyst for other projects including Civic Center Station, the renovated Kitteridge Building, and plans for other mixed-use projects along 16th Street.

More than 90,000 people visit the mall each day to shop, stroll, and relax.

River City Mall

Louisville, Kentucky

Description

River City Mall is located in downtown Louisville, Kentucky, a city with 281,880 residents in a county of 684,638. The mall is located on 4th Avenue and is a transitway that begins at Broadway and continues to River Road for a length of approximately one mile. Fourth Avenue has a right-of-way of 60 feet. The mall, which was originally a three block pedestrian mall 2700 feet long, was renovated beginning in 1986 with construction completed in November 1987 at a cost of $3.1 million. The transitway is eight blocks in length with four blocks exclusively used by the trolley. Expansion to the wharf and other improvements were completed in 1989 at a cost of $1.3 million. The transitway encourages movement between various points along the 2.3 mile loop made by the trolley. The trolleys are patterned after nineteenth-century streetcar design. They are diesel powered, rubber-tired "theme" vehicles called Toonerville II Trolleys. The trolleys are green and decorated with mahogany panels and brass trim. They travel about 15 mph and are heated and air-conditioned. They also have a rear platform where passengers can ride outside in good weather.

The new transitway includes a 22-foot wide transit corridor, pedestrian areas, landscape development of public spaces, trolley stop canopies, signage, lighting, and modification of traffic signals at each intersection.

The original pedestrian mall was accomplished by assessment of property owners for $1.5 million and a HUD grant of $213,000. The mall began in August 1973. The transitway renovation was funded by the Transit Authority of River City (TARC) using Federal Urban Mass Transit money designated for Louisville (80 percent) and local money (20 percent). A portion of the local money was provided by the State of Kentucky, and the remainder came from the TARC Trust Fund. The 1973 pedestrian mall was designed by landscape architects Johnson, Johnson, and Roy, Inc. and the architects were Ryan Associated Architects. The transitway had an initial plan by Barton Aschman Associates with implementation in conjunction with local architects.

Development Strategy

Fourth Avenue, chosen as the location of the pedestrian mall, once been the main commercial area of the downtown. It is presently located between the new riverfront project comprising a hotel, office buildings, and a large plaza, and the downtown core to the south.

The primary purpose of the mall was to revitalize this portion of the downtown. The Louisville Central Area, Inc., composed of 186 property owners, retailers, and financial leaders, met with the mayor, the county judge, the Board of Aldermen, utility companies, and the Louisville Departments of Traffic Engineering and Public Works to initiate the mall project in 1971. The preliminary design was funded by the Louisville Central Area, Inc. The objectives for the mall were as follows:

1. To help stop the decline of land and property values in downtown Louisville.
2. To create a better business climate.
3. To strengthen public confidence in the development of Louisville's downtown core.
4. To give the public a highly usable open space for its own enjoyment.

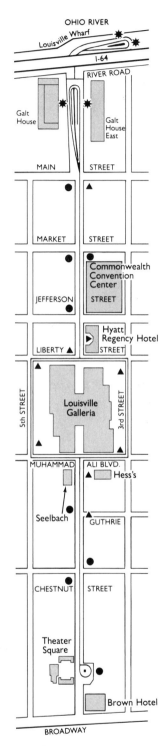

Plan of mall. (Courtesy of City of Louisville Office of Downtown Development.) The 21 trolley stop locations are indicated by the following symbols.
● **Canopy**
▲ **Marker**
✳ **Boarding Sign**

In 1982, after the mall was in place for almost 10 years, a Downtown Action Plan was supported by business and governmental entities. In conjunction with this Action Plan a study was carried out in 1983 that suggested providing a Fourth Avenue shuttle linking the north and south ends of the downtown could spur $6 million in new development. The study's supporters claimed the full pedestrian mall broke the spine of Louisville's downtown business district and deterred new development.

The Transit Authority of River City carried out a Transportation Action Plan for Downtown Louisville in September 1984 and made a report for board members in May 1985. The transitway was approved and construction began in 1986 with funding from the Urban Mass Transportation Authority, State, and TARC Trust Fund. Construction was completed in November 1987 for the first phase and in 1987 for the second phase which extended the transitway to the wharf.

Design Features

River City Mall was designed as "A Place for People." Much attention has been given to human scale, and for those working downtown the mall offers a place filled with people at lunchtime, eating outdoors, meeting friends, and observing others.

Street furnishings are placed in the first 5 feet from the curb, which lines the transitway. The remaining pedestrian areas are left unobstructed.

PAVING
Paving on the pedestrian areas is brick. The transitway itself is paved with bituminous concrete.

PLANTING
Street trees are planted in the walk areas.

SEATING
Wood and iron benches are used on pedestrian areas. There are also raised concrete planters at sitting height.

LIGHTING
Lighting has been redone with turn-of-the-century type fixtures used along the transitway. Banners are also placed on the light poles.

TROLLY STOP CANOPIES
The canopies have smoked glass and are located on each block.

In Retrospect

In the months following completion of the River City Mall in 1973, sales in stores along the mall increased approximately 15 percent according to an information poll taken among the merchants. In 1974, however, the volume of sales decreased, corresponding to the national recession, and in 1975 sales remained constant.

In August 1976, the assessed value of properties along the mall was reduced by 6.5 percent, based on a decrease in revenues produced by the properties.

View of the mall with raised seating and planters, trolley stop, and specially designed trolley. (Photographs courtesy of Lynne Rubenstein.)

A new Galleria shopping center was constructed on 4th Avenue in 1976–1978 in the block between Muhammad Ali Boulevard and Liberty Street. The Galleria has a department store, drugstore, restaurants, food court, and specialty shops. The new trolley transitway loops around the Galleria for one block on 5th Street. The trolley ridership during 1990 was 1,159,518 and was doing quite well. Due to the change of the mall to a transitway the project was rated moderately successful.

The Louisville Central Area is proposing a Management District for a 42-block area of the downtown that includes the transitway, patterned after other successful cities such as Portland and Denver. The goal of the Management District is to enhance the downtown environment. The District will make downtown a more attractive place to work, visit, shop, or locate a business. A program of well-managed supplemental services will enable downtown businesses to ensure their employees of a high-quality, secure environment in which to work. More money will be provided for security, additional cleanup and beautification, marketing, management, and administration for $442,000 per year beginning in January 1992.

View of trolley stop with directory.

Streetscape elements: light poles with banners, iron and wood benches, planters, and pavers.

**Plaza in front of
Galleria adjacent to
the mall.**

**View of Galleria
and its relation to
existing building.**

Mid-America Mall

Memphis, Tennessee

Description

Mid-America Mall is located on Main Street in Memphis, Tennessee, a city with a population of 645,190 residents. The mall stretches 12 blocks (4000 feet) from Exchange Street south to McCall Street. The mall, which was completely pedestrian until February 1991, was about 3000 feet long from Exchange Street to Union Street, where a semimall begins. In late February a complete renovation began with the transformation of the full mall into a transit mall served by an electric trolley rail system. The mall generally has an 85-foot right-of-way, however several areas expand in width, particularly at City Hall. In this location the mall links the Convention Center and auditorium to the principal shopping area. Another large space exists between Jefferson and Madison Streets.

The original mall featured fountains, pools, sculpture, sitting areas, planting, pavilions, kiosks, banners, and performance platforms.

The initial mall was funded by a special tax assessment of property owners. Construction was completed in December 1976, at a cost of $6.7 million. The new transit mall was funded by Urban Mass Transportation Administration set-aside monies along with city, state, and private matching funds. The architects for the full mall were Gassner, Nathan, Browne and the landscape architects were Oliphant and Associates. Architects for the transit mall are Hnedak Bobo Group, P.C.; project engineer, Allen & Hoshall; transportation, Barton-Aschman & Associates; and landscape architect, Toles & Associates.

Development Strategy

The mall was developed to revitalize the central city shopping area. The Downtown Association, an organization of businessmen, was instrumental in promoting the mall in the early 1970s and speakers were invited to give talks on urban design, and several field trips were taken to places such as Atlanta and Minneapolis to see what other cities were doing. A feasibility study funded jointly by the city, county, and businessmen was then carried out by a planning firm. The mall was to be the first step of a total development plan.

Funding for the mall was achieved by creating an assessment district. The city provided funding on an interim basis until money from the assessment was available.

Upon completion it was proclaimed to be the largest urban pedestrian mall of its kind in the United States.

Fifteen years later the paving on the mall was severely damaged due to an unstable subbase, and the entire mall was in need of overall renovation. In 1986 a study was done that recommended a "Mall/Transitway." Light rail was briefly discussed, but discouraged due to little possibility of funding at that time.

Public concern for a transit system sensitive to the environment and new downtown development projects provided the basis for a new study for the Memphis Area Transit Authority (MATA) that would analyze the impact of new development and would focus on an alternative vehicle type such as light rail electrically powered trolleys.

The need for expanding the system to other areas was discussed at public meetings. These areas were the Pyramid/Pinch District, an entertainment/retail area; the South Main Historical District, an arts center; the South Bluffs Development, a mixed-use development that will be residential in character with a hotel and a light commercial district; the Medical Center Complex; St. Jude and St. Joseph Hospital; and Mud Island, since the residential area is growing rapidly on the island north of Auction Bridge and the Harbortown Development is proceeding.

Recommendations were made for

Plan of original mall.

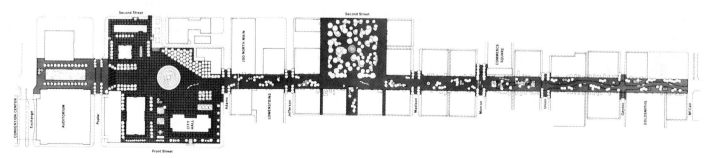

the base system with extensions north to the Pyramid/Pinch District and south to the South Main Historic District and South Bluffs. When IC&G west tracks became available, the development of a River Front Loop became a feasible method of linking the entrance of the Pyramid, an additional 3400 covered parking spaces, the River Front, and the South Bluffs area. The River Front Loop presents a practical transit link, serves as a tourist attraction, and provides linkage to the majority of elements required to make the downtown a viable urban environment. Other recommendations were for the creation of a mall management organization to oversee day-to-day operation of the mall including security, maintenance, and promotion; the maximization of private participation by integrating stations with private development activities along the route; the participation in mall funding by downtown property owners; and the sponsorship of trolley vehicles.

Design Features

PAVING
Materials used for the paving will be concrete and cobbles in the trolley area and brick pavers in the pedestrian areas. The new pavement in conjunction with landscaping will reduce the linear perception of the mall.

PLANTING
In the original mall trees were used to reinforce the auditorium space and to provide shaded sitting areas. Ginko, locust, linden and sycamores were used. Additional landscaping has been added to provide color, texture, shade, and a softer more inviting image.

FOUNTAINS
A new fountain is being designed for the Civic Center area with an interactive design that allows people to move in and out of a "Forest of Water" consisting of 200 20-foot-high plumes of water. A small amphitheater, located at the southeast quadrant of the Plaza, incorporates a backdrop "wall" of water.

LIGHTING
New light poles and fixtures are part of the mall renovation. Lighting concepts illuminate circulation areas, and have been integrated with planting locations to allow building facades to become part of the mall, rather than individual elements.

OTHER ELEMENTS
There is also art on the mall with special feature elements. Special antique

trolleys are being provided to add character to the transit mall. Trolley stop shelters are being constructed, and a pavilion that serves as a trolley stop and information center will be in the Civic Center Plaza area.

In Retrospect

Mid-America Mall provides a 12-block environment that is a people place. The original full mall was con-

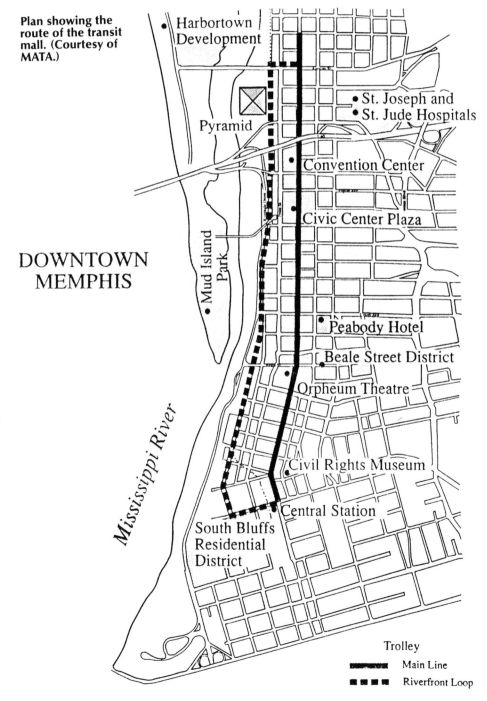

Plan showing the route of the transit mall. (Courtesy of MATA.)

sidered somewhat successful. It has served as an excellent gathering place for workers and residents and also as an ideal staging area for special events and activities. The mall is most popular at lunchtime, but the original design did not draw people into the downtown after working hours. The full mall could have been more user friendly and the quality of construction was not adequate.

Retail sales did not increase over the past 5 years of the full mall, but both property values and assessed rental value increased. There were a number of vacancies above street level, and the mall also did not attract enough tourists or suburban shoppers.

The electric trolley transit mall, with construction beginning in February 1991, will connect into the neighborhoods at either end, and the trolley line will be two miles long. It will link central city areas north to the Pyramid Pinch District and south to the South Main Historic District and the Bluffs. When the IC&G tracks become available the River Front Loop becomes feasible. It provides a linkage to the majority of elements and will help make the downtown a more important urban area. The features on the mall and better construction methods should also help make it successful. The new mall is projected to generate about $685 million of retail construction by the year 2000 with annual property taxes of $19.4 million.

Plan of a prototypical block of the new transit mall. (Courtesy of MATA.)

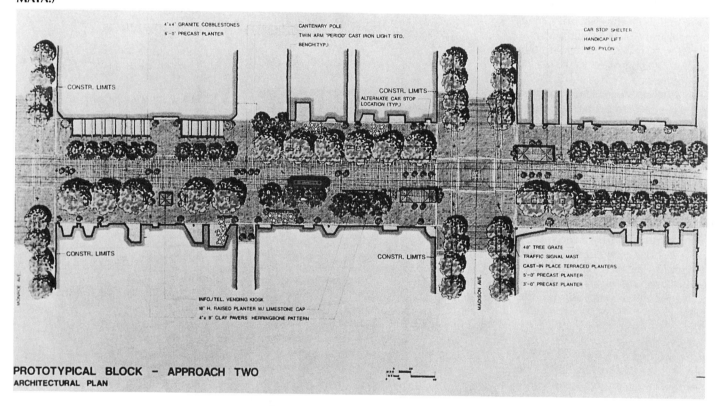

PROTOTYPICAL BLOCK – APPROACH TWO
ARCHITECTURAL PLAN

Nicollet Mall

Minneapolis, Minnesota

Description

Nicollet Mall is located on Nicollet Avenue, the main street of the shopping district in downtown Minneapolis, a city with a population of 344,670. The first phase of the mall, constructed in 1967, was eight blocks (3200 feet) in length with an 80-foot right-of-way. An additional four blocks was added in the second phase.

The mall was renovated in 1990. Nicollet Mall is a transit mall with traffic limited to buses and minibuses that carry shoppers through the length of the shopping district. The original mall had a curvilinear "S" curve serpentine alignment, with a road width of 24 feet. The alignment provided changing motion and a variety of views as one progressed through the mall. The renovated mall has a "C" curve alignment to create wider plaza-like spaces on the wide side of the street. The 1967 mall was designed by landscape architects Lawrence Halprin Associates and planners Barton Aschman Associates. The transit mall renovation was designed by architects BRW, Inc.

The new mall has granite paving, transit shelters, kiosks, two water sculptures, a large pavement artwork, banners, new decorative lights with granite bases, and a performance platform. New sidewalk paving and lights are also provided on side streets from 5th to 11th. Movable and permanent seating are also provided and large evergreen and deciduous trees have been planted. In addition, the mall also has snow melting equipment. The mall has a strong visual terminus to the north at Washington Avenue: the Northwestern National Life Insurance Building.

The initial project was accomplished by funds from an Urban Mass Transportation demonstration grant, an Urban Beautification grant, and a bond issue, to be redeemed by assessments of property located within 330 feet of the mall. The first eight blocks of the mall were completed in November 1967, at a cost of $3.875 million. The renovated mall was funded by the Downtown Business Association and had a cost of $22 million.

Development Strategy

In the mid-1950s Nicollet Avenue was the prime shopping area of the downtown. Shopping centers were under development in suburban areas, however, and positive-thinking individuals formed the Downtown Council in 1955 to improve, expand, and enhance this shopping area. Council members included officers of major corporations, merchants, bankers, property owners, utility companies, and media representatives.

A new planning director was hired, and comprehensive planning, along with a study of the Nicollet area, was begun. The Downtown Council formed a temporary Nicollet Avenue Survey Committee in May 1957. The committee decided that if Nicollet Avenue was improved the impact would be positive throughout the whole downtown. The concept of improving the street was then given high priority by the Downtown Council.

A permanent committee for Nicollet Avenue was formed, and planning consultants were retained to develop a report on the principles and techniques for retail improvement of the street. The report was completed in 1960 and showed that environmental improvement for the street was desirable.

The Planning objectives were as follows:

1. To improve pedestrian circulation.
2. To improve access and encourage mass transportation.
3. To strengthen the identity and image of Nicollet Avenue, thereby creating new opportunities for retail promotion.
4. To encourage private investment by creating a stable environment for retail sales.
5. To develop a transit mall of high aesthetic quality that would link neighborhoods with Nicollet Avenue. All bus routes were to use the mall, cross the mall, or be within one block of the mall.

In 1962 the Downtown Council adopted a plan for the mall that was approved by the City Council and the County Board of Commissioners. The Minneapolis Legislature passed legislation to permit restriction of vehicles on the street and to allow assessment of property owners to help fund the mall. The final assessment plan allotted more than half the total assessment to owners fronting on the mall, while properties off the mall to a distance of 330 feet accounted for the rest. Two benefit zones on the mall and off covered 18 blocks, with each zone having sections providing 100, 100 to 75, 75 to 50, and 50 percent allocations of the cost. The properties closest to the center of the mall paid the greatest proportion of both construction and maintenance expenses. The assessment district provided $2,751,785; the Urban Mass Transportation grant, $512,000; and the Urban Beautification grant, $483,500. Private utility companies cooperated by agreeing to check their lines and update them as necessary so that disturbance to the street in the future would be minimal. Utility costs were $2.5 million.

When the bid for construction of the mall came in high, the city decided to

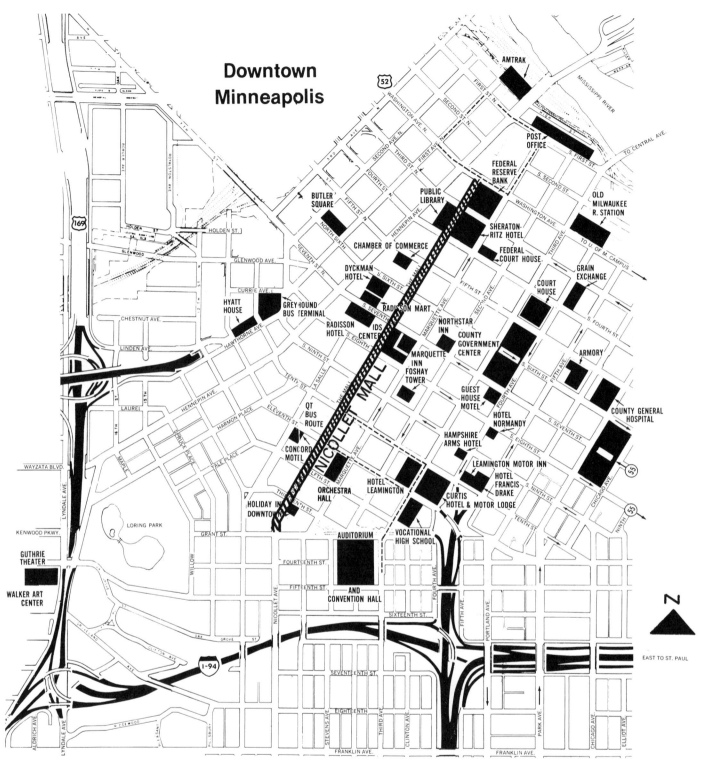

Downtown Minneapolis

Mall location plan.

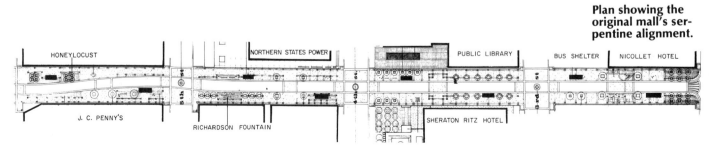

Plan showing the original mall's serpentine alignment.

act as general contractor for the project.

Renovated Mall

In July 1986 a Committee on the Future of Nicollet Mall was formed to rethink the mall. The Committee was staffed by the Minneapolis Planning Department, The Downtown Development Task Force, the City's Department of Public Works, the Minneapolis Community Development Agency, The Metropolitan Transit Commission, and the Downtown Council.

Goals and Strategy

GOALS

The primary goal was to make the central business district, as anchored by Nicollet Mall, the central shopping place in the Twin Cities and the Upper Midwest region, as well as the city itself.

The secondary goal was to serve customers, residents, and employees in the core and primary trade areas by meeting a significant portion of their retail needs. A major objective was to increase the mall area's share of regional retail sales by at least 25 percent with a minimum of $318 million in additional retail sales by the year 2000.

STRATEGY

The strategy to carry out the primary goal was as follows:

1. Create a unique combination of shopping opportunities not available elsewhere in the Twin Cities and Upper Midwest region.
2. Provide exciting nonretail facilities such as restaurants, entertainment, public spaces, streetscapes, and special events.
3. Provide ease of access—transit, automobile, parking, and pedestrian.
4. Develop creative use of the arts, open space, and streetscape to reinforce the mall.
5. Provide strong linkages to the rest of downtown with the mall as the focus. Nonretail and retail uses are mixed giving the entire area a sense of excitement and diversity.

The secondary goal may be carried out by serving the core and primary area shoppers by expanding the base of moderate to budget retail opportunities. These opportunities will not dominate the retail mix, but will be an important part of the overall retail facilities.

Form

FORM

Retail is generally located in a multilevel linear pattern along both sides of the mall for approximately six blocks from 5th to 11th Streets.

PEDESTRIAN MOVEMENT

A system of sidewalks and second level skyways was created that is integrated and supportive of retail activity, comfortable in all seasons, and understandable to visitors and frequent shoppers. This was accomplished by the following:

1. Reconstructing the street level.
2. Improving access from the street to skyways making the connections easy and apparent.
3. Retrofiting and expanding the skyway system within the retail core.

TRANSIT AND CARS

The mall was designed as an exclusive transitway without the use of cars by the following:

1. Making the mall a destination and bringing people to it.
2. Minimizing negative effects such as noise and exhaust.
3. Making transit an amenity or attraction to users.
4. Helping achieve retail and pedestrian movement objectives.

CLIMATE CONTROL

The mall is special as a retail area because it provides shoppers with a choice regarding climate control, which should be preserved. These elements include

1. Heated sidewalks for snow melting.
2. Skyways.
3. Transit shelters.

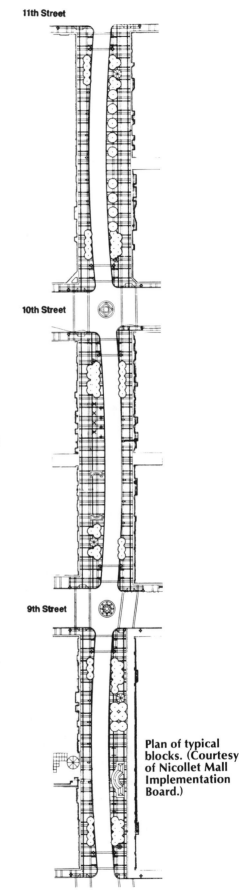

11th Street

10th Street

9th Street

Plan of typical blocks. (Courtesy of Nicollet Mall Implementation Board.)

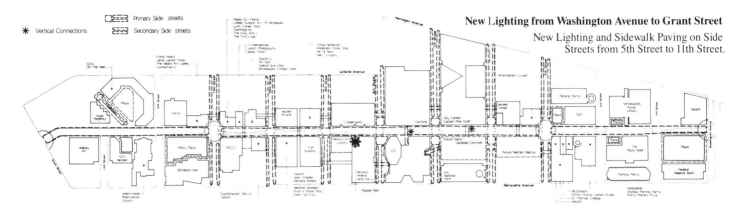

New Lighting from Washington Avenue to Grant Street

New Lighting and Sidewalk Paving on Side Streets from 5th Street to 11th Street.

Plan showing the overall mall areas planned for new lighting. (Courtesy of Nicollet Mall Implementation Board.)

View of 1967 mall design. (Photograph courtesy of Downtown Council of Minneapolis.)

THE STREET AND RETAIL

The retail and main street functions can and should be mutually supportive. Public amenities and activities—transit, street furniture, art, etc.—will create an environment that supports retail. The Nicollet Mall, both street and retail, will be inviting, comfortable, and of the highest quality. The mall's design will symbolize its role as the prominent shopping center of the Upper Midwest.

Supportive Elements

PARKING

Plan, implement, and manage a downtown parking and transportation system that ensures availability and convenience of shopper parking. Parking will be

1. Easy to get to from the freeway and street system.
2. Understandable by both the frequent and occasional user.
3. Safe.
4. Attractive.
5. Predictable.

The Mall Implementation Board will recommend a means to ensure that parking is available and affordable to potential mall customers.

So that parking for shoppers is not preempted by downtown employees, a comprehensive transportation strategy must be pursued, including

1. Completion of peripheral parking.
2. Linkage of peripheral parking ramps to the core area by skyways.
3. Increased parking requirements for office use in downtown's outer core.

4. Parking requirements in downtown's peripheral areas equal to the parking demand.
5. An improved transit system.

The use of street level mall property for parking lots should be prohibited or discouraged.

TRANSIT

1. Location should be on and/or below the Nicollet Mall in order to
   a. Maintain the capacity and attractiveness of transit as an option.
   b. Serve city residents with the desire or need to use public transit.
   c. Add activity to the mall environment.
2. Provision for Light Rail Transit in the future.
3. Intradowntown transit on the mall.

View of the curved area of the mall during construction. (Photograph courtesy of BRW, Inc.)

The Nicollet Mall Implementation Board should recommend the best method for trips from the Convention Center to Riverplace. Alternatives should include

1. A special fare zone.
2. A major shuttle system.
3. A combination of a special fare zone with some shuttle vehicles.
4. A specially designed vehicle for shoppers and workers.

Improved off peak transit service, transit at grade—buses or a special shuttle should remain at grade.

ENTERTAINMENT AND CULTURAL FACILITIES

Major entertainment, sports, and cultural facilities should be located in close proximity and connected to the mall with street level retail, public spaces, amenities, and skyways.

1. Strong pedestrian links should be provided between entertainment uses and Nicollet Mall retail by attractive and comfortable street level uses along the cross-streets and with the skyway system.
2. The Convention Center, headquarters hotel, and supportive parking should be linked with the mall retail by a streetscape system and by skyways.
3. Cultural and sports facilities add to the unique quality of the downtown and its attraction as a place to spend leisure time with facilities such as art galleries. These facilities should be encouraged near the retail core.

OFFICE

A strong relationship exists between downtown offices and shopping. About 70 percent of employee shoppers work within five blocks of where they shop. A compact downtown should continue to be pursued. The highest density office should occur in the inner core.

HOUSING

Housing should be encouraged in the downtown. It provides activity during the evenings and on weekends that tends to make the entire central business area more secure and attractive for visitors and other users.

Management and Marketing

MANAGEMENT

Nicollet Mall will be managed as an integrated whole. Management will tie pieces of the avenue together with promotional activities, special events, street activity, maintenance, and operation. This will reinforce the mall's special urban character, diversity, and excitement.

View of mall and its street furnishings. (Photograph courtesy of BRW, Inc.)

Nicollet Avenue will be linked to and integrated with the whole downtown in a mutually beneficial relationship. A central organization will be created to manage and market the retail core.

Implementation

The City Council received the report of the Committee on the Future of Nicollet Mall, which was completed in December 1986. Implementation of construction began in April 1990. The budget for the mall was $22 million, funded by the Downtown Business Association.

Design Features

The mall is of high quality and durable materials are used such as granite. The linear plazas alternate from side to side allowing more space in wider areas for entertainment stages and movable objects such as vendors carts.

PAVING

The paving on the renovated mall is granite in a series of pink, red, and gray rectilinear grids. There is over 150,000 square feet of granite installed with a flame finish surface. The pavers are 2¼ inch thick ranging in size from one to three foot square.

TRANSIT SHELTERS

The shelters are glass enclosures 12 feet in diameter placed on the wide side of each block.

KIOSKS

Kiosks are 6 feet in diameter with the outside containing a mall directory, mall map, skyway map, event panel, and telephone.

SEATING

Permanent and movable seating will be used on the mall for flexibility. Seating will also be built into feature elements such as the performance platforms.

LIGHTING

New lighting was designed for the mall. A white high-efficiency light source is being provided. The lights have a granite base with the minimum of one lantern. At cross streets a lantern and four globes are used, on Nicollet Avenue a lantern and two globes are used, and on side streets a lantern is also used. New lighting is designed from Washington Avenue to Grant Street with new lighting on sidewalk paving for side streets from 5th to 11th Street.

BANNER POLES

Banner poles have built in lighting for convention and special events.

View of granite paving, night lighting, and flower pots. (Photograph courtesy of BRW, Inc.)

ART WORK

Two water sculptures and a large pavement art work are also planned.

PLANTING

Ninety-eight 18- to 20-foot-high Austrian Pines trimmed from the pavement up to 7½ feet to allow walking beneath were planted. The trees have 6-foot-high tree guards and tree grates. In addition 33 Lindens were installed north of 5th Street and south of 10th Street, six White Oaks were planted in front of Carsons, and four Ginkos were planted facing the Conservatory.

OTHER AMENITIES

The new mall has linear plazas that alternate from side to side. This allows more movable objects such as

vendor carts, entertainment stages, and the farmers market. New signage is also being designed for the mall.

In Retrospect

Nicollet Mall is regarded as very successful since its completion in 1967. Pedestrian traffic increased, and there was also an increase in retail sales of about 14 percent. The mall acted as a catalyst and more than $225 million of new construction or rehabilitation was completed along the transitway.

The IDS Center, a 57-story structure octagonal in shape, built at a cost of $125 million, has 2.25 million square feet. Completed in 1973, it contains an office, hotel, bank, gallery, theatre, and underground parking.

The mall has also helped to strengthen other areas of the downtown. The impact of the mall has

spread beyond its immediate area to improve the regional center and its environs, thereby gaining a national image.

A system of skyway links at the second story level began in 1962. Over the years the skyway system began to drain pedestrian traffic away from the retail stores on the ground level and in the early 1980s one department store moved and another was destroyed by fire.

Since 1988 Saks Fifth Avenue and two specialty retail centers have opened with Neiman Marcus following. The new $22 million renovation that began in 1990 will also give the mall added strength for the future and help it achieve its goal to make the central business as anchored by the mall, the central shopping place in the Twin Cities and the Upper Midwest.

View of banners with Austrian Pine trees in the background. (Photograph courtesy of BRW, Inc.)

Chestnut Street Transitway

Philadelphia, Pennsylvania

Description

The Chestnut Street Transitway is located along one of Philadelphia's busiest downtown shopping streets in a city with a population of 1,647,000. The transitway mall is 12 blocks long, stretching from 6th to 18th Streets. Generally, the mall is 60 feet in width, but between 9th and 10th Streets it is wider because of the setback of federal buildings. Traffic on the transitway is limited to buses on a 20-foot-wide roadway. After 6:00 P.M. taxicabs are allowed. Automobiles are allowed on the mall from 6:30 P.M. until 6:00 A.M.

The mall is a shopping promenade and features expanded sidewalks, pedestrian crosswalks at midblock, specially designed lighting with bicentennial theme elements attached to light standards, bus shelters, raised planters, and some seating. The transitway was designed by architects and planners Ueland and Junker, engineers DeLeuw, Cather, and landscape architectural consultant Eugene De Sillets. Efficient transit was a dominant goal of the development plans, and so application was made for federal funding. The project was funded by the Urban Mass Transportation Administration, the city, and the state. The transitway was completed in June 1976, at a cost of $7.4 million.

Development Strategy

In the mid-1960s, the city government had feasibility studies made on turning Chestnut Street into a pedestrian mall. The Chestnut Street Association, founded by merchants on and near the street, voiced strong objections, and the concept was not developed further.

However, the following decade was marked by an increasing number of middle-class residents commuting to work, a fuel crisis, and shifting urban patterns that resulted in heavier use of the public transit system. Merchants began changing their attitudes toward upgrading Chestnut Street, and city officials approached them with the concept of a transit mall.

Also, Philadelphia '76, Inc., the city's bicentennial organization, was seeking transportation alternatives to move visitors easily between the historic area, on the east side of center city, and the permanent museums along the Benjamin Franklin Parkway to the west.

Architects worked on a concept with Philadelphia '76, Inc., and were then retained by a committee of Chestnut Street merchants to develop the design of the transit mall. In March 1974, the plan was approved by the general membership of the Chestnut Street Association, even though some opposition was voiced by parking lot owners along the street, who feared that their businesses would suffer from removal of automobile traffic.

Funding was approved by the Urban Mass Transportation Administration for 80 percent of the $7.4 million cost. The remainder was split by the city and the state.

The city and bicentennial officials promised merchants that construction of the mall would not disrupt Christmas shopping and that it would be completed by April 1976. When the street was closed to traffic and construction began, there were few problems. Traffic studies showed that Market Street had unused capacity and could handle much of the rerouted traffic. Also, parking was banned for a block in either direction on streets intersecting with Chestnut to allow service zones for truck delivery. Some nighttime loading is allowed on the transitway by special permit.

Design Features

PAVING
Walks have been increased to 20 feet in width on each side of the roadway. Sidewalk areas are paved predominantly in brick, with concrete adjacent to building facades and in the crosswalk pattern at midblock. Curbs fade out at crosswalk areas for ease of pedestrian use.

LIGHTING
Night lighting was specially designed for the mall. Clusters of eight luminous globes of smoky gray acrylic plastic are placed on 14-foot-high anodized bronze aluminum poles. Bicentennial elements were also attached to the tops of the poles.

Other illumination is provided by high level lights on 28-foot poles. These lights use 400-watt high pressure sodium lamps. There are also lights included in the pedestrian signals at midblock areas.

BUS SHELTERS
Large, transparent, roofed bus shelters are provided. They are free standing and take up minimal space both physically and visually.

PLANTING
Trees are planted both directly in the sidewalk areas and in raised tree planters. Grates are used around the trees placed in walk areas.

SEATING
Benches in a small sitting area are provided in conjunction with the midblock crosswalk area. These benches are limited to about four per block. Trash receptacles are also placed near the benches (perhaps too close), as well as in other locations.

In Retrospect

The transitway has improved pedestrian circulation on Chestnut Street with an increase in foot traffic. In a survey of merchants in late 1985, in which 77 forms were returned of 247 distributed, 46 percent had a favorable attitude toward the transitway, 27 percent were indifferent, and 27 percent had an unfavorable attitude.

Of 1800 questionnaires passed out to the public along the transitway in 1985, 71 percent believed Chestnut Street is better with the transitway, 17 percent believed it would be better without it, and 12 percent had no opinion.

Overall the quality of establishments has declined along one-third to one-half of the transitway. The City, however, hopes to extend the transit-way east toward Penn's Landing and west to the 30th Street Station with service for trains and subways. Also, a new Special Service District began in 1991. The District is located around the transitway and will have a positive effect on mall security and management. The City also envisions renovation of curbs, sidewalks, and other street furnishings as funds become available. Particularly needed

Typical view of mall. (Photograph courtesy of Rohm and Haas Company.)

View of crosswalk area at midblock, including traffic controls. (Photograph courtesy of Rohm and Haas Company.)

A 24-inch clear Plexiglas cube is placed on each traffic control column. Each cube contains a 50-watt mercury vapor lamp. (Photograph courtesy of Rohm and Haas Company.)

are more and better seating areas with attention to the location of these areas.

Rental rates and property values increased through 1989, but have been stable or declined to date. Although other development has occurred nearby there are no data to indicate it was generated because of the transitway. Overall, the mall has been somewhat successful as shown from surveys of merchants along the transitway.

Sitting areas. (Photograph courtesy of Rohm and Haas Company.)

View of crosswalk and sidewalk areas. (Photograph courtesy of Ueland and Junker.)

Portland Transit Mall

Portland, Oregon

Description

The Portland Transit Mall is located on 5th and 6th Avenues in downtown Portland, Oregon, a city with 418,470 residents. The mall is 11 blocks (2800 feet) in length on each avenue for a total of 22 blocks. The streets have an 80-foot right-of-way with each block 260 feet to the centerline of cross streets. The mall begins at Madison Street and proceeds north to Burnside. This transit mall has two bus lanes and one automobile lane in all but 6 of the 22 blocks. The purpose of the mall is to help eliminate automobiles from a major portion of the central business district by acting as the hub of a regional transit system. The project also assists in improving air quality by providing a 60 percent reduction of air pollutants in the downtown.

The mall features new paving, fountains, sculpture, kiosks, bus shelters, sitting areas, comfort stations, and traffic signalization. The mall architects were Skidmore, Owings, and Merrill, the landscape architects were Lawrence Halprin and Associates, and

the engineers, Moffat, Nichols, and Bonney. The transit mall was funded by the Urban Mass Transportation Administration and by Tri-Met, the local transit agency. The project was completed in November 1977, at a cost of $15 million.

Development Strategy

Before December 1969 private carriers served Portland's mass transport needs. Between 1950 and 1970, however, a sizable decrease occurred in the number of commuters using mass transit. By 1960 persons using mass transit constituted only 19 percent of commuters, and by 1970 only 15 percent. Numerically, the decrease was from 45,000 in 1950 to 20,000 in 1970. Commuters, on the other hand, increased by 50,000.

In 1969 Tri-Met became the principal operator of the transit system. The city of Portland developed a downtown plan, announced in 1972, that called for a transit mall along 5th and 6th Avenues. The Portland City Planning Commission approved the

mall concept, and the City Council endorsed it in January 1972. This followed the Urban Mass Transportation Administration's approval for partial financing of a preliminary study of the mall. Tri-Met selected a team of consultants to develop a preliminary design. Several alternative designs were studied. The scheme chosen has two exclusive bus lanes through the mall with a third lane for automobile use in 16 of the 22 blocks. If volume of transit traffic increases as expected, the third lane will also be used for one of the following:

1. Buses in the third lane in the opposite direction.
2. Shuttles or special route buses.
3. Continuation of buses on the mall as originally planned.
4. Use of high capacity vehicles such as fixed guideway or light rail in the left lane.

The mall was funded by the Urban Mass Transportation Administration for 80 percent of its cost and by Tri-Met for the remainder.

**Plan of mall.
(Photographs courtesy of Tri-Met.)**

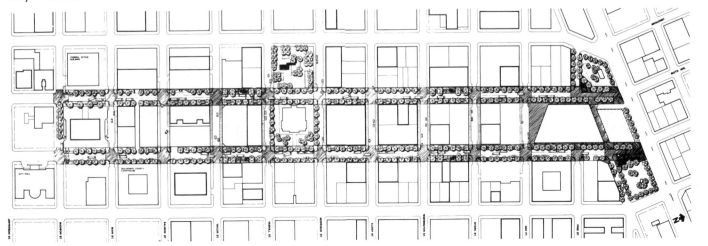

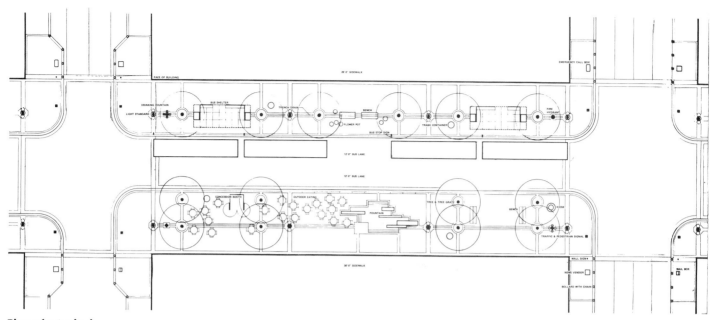

Plan of a typical
block.

View looking down
on the transit mall
with its street tree
plantings.

View of streetscape
elements including
lighting, banner
poles, bollards, and
fountain.

Design Features

The mall was designed to be inviting to residents and visitors, to be beneficial to downtown businesses, and to encourage an alternative to the use of automobiles. Street furnishings were designed to be complementary in form and materials.

FOUNTAINS
Six large fountains are placed at entrances to the mall at Burnside Street, on 5th and 6th, and between State and Washington, and Yamhill and Taylor, where the automobile lane is replaced by wider pedestrian areas.

PAVING
The transit mall features a composition of textures, colors, and natural and man-made materials.

One material used is brick in a herringbone pattern on sidewalks and pedestrian zones. Brick also defines borders around trees, light standards, and intersections. Concrete is used in other areas, along with granite for curbs and gutters. Tree grates, also part of the pattern, are made of cast iron.

LIGHTING
Some of Portland's old lighting standards are used to add a unique character and a continuity with the city's past. New crystal spheres replace the old globes. These lights have a 20-foot height. There is also low lighting in bollards at midblock.

PLANTING
The planting design has 250 London plane trees along the avenues. At least six trees have been placed on each side of every block.

BENCHES
Benches are at midblock locations. They have a double curve of wood slats banded with bronzed metal at the center and ends. The benches face in two directions perpendicular to the street.

BOLLARDS
Granite bollards connected by bronzed chains are placed at each intersection. They indicate to pedestrians where the mall begins and guide them to crossings.

KIOSKS AND CONCESSION BOOTHS
Communication, display, and small merchandising facilities are placed along the mall. These provide places for announcements, exhibits, and refreshments, and to ease in use of the mall. The concession booths, of two sizes, are used for the sale of flowers, newspapers, and snacks.

SIGNALS AND SIGNS
New 13.5-foot-high traffic signals are also used on the mall. They have bronze-colored metal supports and illuminated graphics. In addition, there are police and fire call boxes on the mall.

CLOCKS
Clocks are placed on the old lamp standards. Four of these are used along the mall. Each clock has four faces and has a height of about 16 feet.

View of brick paving and flower pots along transit mall.

211

BUS SHELTERS

These shelters are transparent pavilions constructed of components similar to those used in the rest of the mall. For protection from wind and rain they are open only on the street side. Bronze-colored metal is used for the structural system.

In Retrospect

The transit mall has helped to revitalize the downtown and has been a catalyst for development, attracting more than $1 billion in private funds for projects including Pioneer Place, which began in March 1988. The $121 million project developed by Rouse has retail and commercial facilities with Saks Fifth Avenue, a new hotel, and a gallery of shops and offices on four square blocks in the heart of downtown. Bordered by the mall on 5th Avenue, it is one of the most transit intensive developments in the country. Travel time has also been cut in half through the downtown and now takes 15 minutes.

Retail sales for the mall have increased in the past 5 years as have property values and assessed rental value. The mall is considered very successful.

Lovejoy and Civic Center Forecourt Fountains

As part of the pedestrian circulation system, the mall is only a short distance from the Lovejoy and Civic Center Forecourt Fountains, a few blocks to the south. These fountains, especially the Civic Center Forecourt Fountain, are very spectacular and draw numerous people who enjoy watching them and participating in wading, sunbathing, and lounging. The fountains are built of concrete.

Specially designed bus shelters are provided along the transit mall.

Drinking fountain
as a streetscape
element.

Lovejoy Fountain,
Portland, Oregon.

**View of Civic
Center Forecourt,
Portland, Oregon.**

Granville Mall

*Vancouver, British
Columbia, Canada*

Description

Granville Mall is a transit mall located in Vancouver, British Columbia, a city of 426,502 residents. It was planned to facilitate pedestrian use in a six-block (3000-feet) area along Granville Street from Nelson to Hastings. Granville Street, which had six lanes of traffic with 1200 vehicles per hour, was reduced to two lanes of traffic with 100 buses per hour. Pedestrian walks were widened to as much as 35 feet, hundreds of large trees were planted, new paving was installed, and incandescent street lights were added in the first phase. In the second phase, sitting areas, bus shelters, and additional lighting were added. The mall was designed by architects Bain, Burroughs, Hanson, and Raimet. The transit mall was accomplished with funds from assessment of property owners, the Federal Winter Works Program, British Columbia Hydro, and the city. Phase One was completed in August 1974, and Phase Two in September 1976. The cost of the project was $3 million.

Development Strategy

The primary purpose of the mall was to revitalize Granville Street, which was rapidly deteriorating. The design was to facilitate pedestrian use and act as a framework for redevelopment, along with creating a safer, quieter environment for people to enjoy shopping, business, theatres, and walking. Granville Street was always an important street, with its theatre row, banking, small shops, and department stores. By the latter 1960s, however, shoppers seemed to have abandoned the narrow sidewalks and noisy streets for shopping centers. The situation deteriorated until merchants petitioned the City

Council to take action, and in the summer of 1972 a series of meetings was held between the city's Social Planning Department and police force and people concerned about Granville.

It was decided that because of Granville's historical importance and its role as a gateway to the downtown, it was important to provide a long-term solution to the various social, business, and environmental problems of the street. A special joint committee made up of both city staff and City Council was established to study the feasibility of a mall. It was thought that a transit mall would be best. There were several reasons why the merchants wanted buses to be kept on the street. The primary reason was that access to stores would be maintained and that buses would encourage pedestrian flow. If a new transit system is installed, buses can be removed to make the mall completely pedestrian oriented.

The prototype for the Granville Mall was the Nicollet Mall in Minneapolis, which the city's task force on mall feasibility visited in August 1973.

On September 25, 1973, the City Council approved the mall design by the consulting architect. A tight deadline of 12 months was set for Phase One, and methods had to be worked out to adhere to the schedule.

Policies relating to street vending, cafes, signs, loading, and street use were also determined.

Funding for the mall was as follows: property owners, $900,000; the Federal Winter Works Program, $543,000; British Columbia Hydro, $165,000; and the city, $1,338,560.

SIGNS
Although many other cities with malls have tried to discourage or prohibit projecting signs, this change is

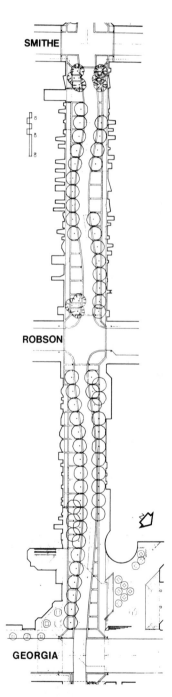

Plan of typical block on mall. (Photographs courtesy of Bain, Burroughs, Hanson, and Raimet.)

215

not contemplated for the Granville Mall. The Sign Bylaw was used to encourage awnings and canopies; other bright projecting signs, including theatre marquees, were allowed to continue in order to maintain some of the character that had developed on the street.

ZONING

Zoning was amended to make the street more pleasant for pedestrians and to stop deterioration. Banks and financial institutions were limited to 25 feet of frontage on the mall because of the dead space often created by nonretail facilities. Massage parlors were controlled by making them conditional use areas that must be approved by the Development Permit Board.

STREET VENDING

A Street Vending Bylaw was enacted, providing for licenses to be issued for specific locations distributed along the mall. Permits were issued to encourage a variety of goods on the mall. Special vendors' kiosks were also designed.

CAFES

A set of simple guidelines was prepared to encourage the development of sidewalk cafes by restaurant owners.

CITIZEN PARTICIPATION

No association concerned with Granville Street existed before the mall was constructed. First, an interim committee of merchants from each of the six blocks was appointed. This group then held elections and became the Granville Business Association. Through its membership fees, the association has developed programming events on the mall. During the summer of 1975, many cultural events were scheduled, including a series of "Mozart on the Mall" concerts, art and photographic exhibits, and puppet shows.

Design Features

In the first phase of development, basic elements such as trees, paving, and lighting were installed. The second phase included sitting areas, additional lighting, bus shelters, and other amenities.

PLANTING

Tree-lined streets are an important feature in Vancouver. Therefore trees became the major focus and unifying element of the design and are used to define entrances to streets, to give a sense of separation of pedestrian areas from the transitway, and to create spaces for special activities. Over 200 trees, many of them with trunks 4 to 5 inches in caliper, were used on the mall. Beech trees were planted in the greatest number, with red maple, European ash, purple leaf birch, western hemlock, dogwood, vine maple, Oregon grape, and Scotch pine trees also used.

STREET LIGHTING

Incandescent street lighting on early Vancouver lamp standards provides a feeling of warmth. There are also two lights at the base of each tree, along with outlets for special use. These outlets can be used to connect Christmas decorations.

View of mall looking southwest from the corner of Georgia and Granville.

SEATING
Raised concrete and wood benches are arranged in groups around trees.

PAVING
Paving is a light-colored exposed aggregate concrete.

CAFES
Restaurant owners are granted permission to set up Parisian-style sidewalk cafes, with canopies and glass enclosures for inclement weather.

OTHER FURNISHINGS
These include bus shelters and specially designed vendors' kiosks.

In Retrospect

In 1975 the assessed rental value of properties along the mall increased by about $636,000 over 1974 figures. A business tax revenue gain of over $60,000 (8 percent) was realized in 1975.

The mall's performance was particularly impressive in the 900 block, in which the rate of decay was worse before construction. Assessed rental values increased 50 percent from $300,000 in 1974 to $450,000 in 1975. This generated business tax revenues of $43,021, an increase of $14,250 for the block. In 1975 the assessed rental value for the 900 block of Granville, $452,850, equaled the revenue of the 1000 block of Robson Street, a most prestigious block.

View looking northeast from the lower end of mall. Winding streets provide a variety of pedestrian spaces.

Sitting areas at corner of Georgia and Granville.

Detail of sitting area and lighting for tree.

View of vendor's kiosk.

View of bus shelter.

218

Over the past 5 years retail sales have not increased, however, property values have risen and assessed rental value has also increased on some blocks.

The transit mall has been an effective transit corridor. Movie theatres have concentrated on Robson Street to Smithe, which has continued to grow as a strong theatre area.

Private traffic was added to one of the six blocks. The City Council voted to open the 900 block to traffic in February 1988 after much discussion. This was done to improve traffic flow, for proposed new uses in the block, and because of the high number of vacancies. Overall, the mall is considered somewhat successful.

**View of Market
Street Mall,
Wilmington,
Delaware.**

(preceding pages)

**View of Bayside,
Miami.**

8

Comparative Analysis of Pedestrian Malls

The three types of pedestrian malls were reviewed to see how they had fared over the past 5 years or more. A survey was sent to each city to obtain data related to changes in the form of the mall, its economic success, its help in generating other retail development or revitalization, and the overall general degree of the mall's success.

TRANSIT MALLS

Of the mall categories, the transit malls with their related urban streetscape treatment seem to be the most successful as a group. The transit malls surveyed were in large cities of about 350,000 to 1,650,000 residents. The cost of these malls was significant as shown in Table 8-1.

Pedestrian uses and transit uses seem to complement each other, and in a few cases some of the transit malls have limited automobile traffic during the evening, on one block, or in one lane. Examples of this are the evening automobile traffic on Philadelphia's Chestnut Street Transitway, one block of private transit on Vancouver's Granville Mall, and one lane of general traffic for three-quarters of the blocks in Portland's Transit Mall.

In some cases the transitways were designed primarily as transportation facilities such as in Portland and Denver, which bring people into the city from suburban or residential areas. These transitways provide a corridor or link through a variety of land uses including retail, office core, and in some places entertainment. In Memphis, Tennessee the original full mall on 12 blocks is being converted to an electric trolley transit mall that will extend for two miles with residential neighborhoods at each end. Pedestrian and transit uses comple-

TABLE 8-1 Transit Malls/Transitways

LOCATION AND NAME	DATE COMPLETED	COST/ BLOCKS	TRANSIT TYPES	FUNDING TYPES	LAND USER AREAS	BENEFITS	DEGREE OF SUCCESS
Denver, Colorado 16 Street Mall	1982	$29,000,000 13 Blocks	Shuttle buses	UMTA Capital Grant	Retail core	Improve retail, traffic, congestion	Very successful as free transit shuttle
				Regional Transportation District	Offices	Reduce pollution	Somewhat successful as a catalyst No sales increase last 5 years
Louisville, Kentucky River City Mall	1973	$1,713,000 Full mall 3 Blocks		Assessment Urban renewal and bonds			
	1987 Transitway renovation	$4,400,000 Transitway 8 Blocks	Diesel trolley	UMTA funds State funds TARC trust fund	Retail Office Entertainment Waterfront	Improve retail, transit	Moderately successful
Philadelphia, Pennsylvania Chestnut Street Transitway	1976	$7,400,000 12 Blocks	Transit buses Tourist buses Taxis one block day Emergency vehicles General traffic 6:30 P.M. to 6:00 A.M.	UMTA Capital Grant State DOT City Capital Funds	Retail core Offices	Retail Transit for bicentennial	Somewhat successful Improve transit
Portland, Oregon Portland Transit Mall	1977	$15,000,000 22 Blocks	Transit buses General traffic on one lane for ¾ of blocks	UMTA Capital Grant TRI-MET Utilities by city depts. and utility companies	Office core Intersects retail core	Increased transit use and improve efficiency Improve retail and pedestrian streetscape environment Sales increase during past 5 years	Very successful
Vancouver, British Columbia, Canada Granville Mall	1974	$2,947,000 6 Blocks	Transit buses Private vehicles added to one block	Property owners Federal City Utilities	Retail Office core Entertain- ment	Improve transit Improve street- scape Effective transit corridor	Somewhat successful
Memphis, Tennessee Mid-America Mall	1976	$6,000,000 Full mall		Full mall had tax assess- ments	Retail	Revitalized downtown	Somewhat successful as a full mall
	1991 Transit mall renovation	$33,000,000 Transit mall 12 Blocks	Electric trolley	UMTA Capital Grant City, state and private matching funds	Office	Property value and assessed rental value increased	

TABLE 8-1 (*Continued*)

LOCATION AND NAME	DATE COMPLETED	COST/ BLOCKS	TRANSIT TYPES	FUNDING TYPES	LAND USER AREAS	BENEFITS	DEGREE OF SUCCESS
Minneapolis, Minnesota Nicollet Mall	1967	$3,875,000 8 Blocks Phase 1 4 Blocks Phase 2	Transit buses Shuttle buses Taxis Emergency vehicles	Assessment district UMTA Demonstration Grant Urban Beautification Grant	Retail Office	Retail and bus service Image Streetscape	Very successful
	1990–1991 renovation	$22,000,000 12 Blocks	Transit buses Shuttle buses	Downtown Business Association	Entertainment		

ment each other in these larger cities, where neither pedestrian nor transit volumes alone could justify removal of a street from automobile use; together they do. The transit mall is a good solution, which may be better than closing a block completely to traffic and can help improve transit while also providing a place for people and an identifiable image for a city. It also helps to satisfy many merchants who feel that some vehicular activity creates vitality that is important for their business success.

FULL MALLS

Full pedestrian malls are a much different approach to downtown revitalization than transit malls. Full malls, although very popular in the 1960s and 1970s, are harder to justify today in terms of economic viability.

In the malls surveyed, whereas several were somewhat to very successful, a few were unsuccessful and have been or are in the process of being reopened to automobile traffic (see Table 8-2).

Many downtown retail areas had problems because people lived and shopped mostly in suburban areas that were not only more convenient but provided free parking and had a greater diversity of merchandise. Downtown areas on the other hand had two groups for support, the lunchtime office workers and in many cases the lower income city residents. From economic market studies a decline of retail sales on a mall

reflects a decline within the overall central business district. Some of the pedestrian malls that got started early before shopping malls were established were able to compete better with the suburban shopping areas. Also, important for success was the number of office workers and others close to the mall such as college students. Only about 20 percent of shoppers will walk more than 9 minutes or about three blocks during a 1-hour lunch break. Also, new locations for development have taken place outside the immediate downtown core on land that is less expensive. These new office and/or retail facilities have lured business away from the original central city core. Where these conditions exist it may not matter how well the original pedestrian mall was planned or maintained.

For downtowns to be successful there must be a competitive mix of merchandising, new activity generators to draw people to the downtown, and linkage of the downtown's major attractions such as cultural facilities, conference, hotel, and office uses, and entertainment and residential facilities.

Special character and recognizability of the downtown including historic buildings, quality streetscapes, convenient reasonably priced parking, ease of mass-transit use by bus, subway, or train, and maintenance and security are important. Some cities such as Charlottesville, Virginia have had very successful full malls that actually increased in size as shown in Table 8-2. Other cities have gone through periods of change in their

malls. Some of the malls that were originally full malls have had one or more blocks opened to automobile traffic. This evolution based on specific needs in an urban area need not be viewed negatively. In Europe, many of the downtown spaces evolved over hundreds of years. Carefully done economic and planning studies may provide strong reasons for selecting one type of mall versus another, since each city has its own identity and personality.

SEMIMALLS

The semimall in effect is a streetscape where sidewalks have been widened for ease of use by pedestrians, and in many cases parking spaces have been reduced or completely eliminated. The semimall may be a good choice for a downtown, especially in smaller cities. It allows good visibility of retail facilities and provides greater activity from the combination of both pedestrians and automobiles. The semimall can provide visual continuity in the downtown by use of materials and furnishings including street trees that produce a harmonious streetscape and develop an image for the downtown. The highest quality material for paving and furnishings within the budget should be selected. Quality materials provide a good image and will last for a longer time with less funds needed for repair. Maintenance and security are also high priority items in the overall management of the retail core. If one looks at the suburban malls they generally are

TABLE 8-2 Full Malls and Semimalls

LOCATION AND NAME	DATE COMPLETED	COST	TYPE	BLOCK LENGTH	FUNDING TYPES	PHYSICAL CHANGES SINCE CONSTRUCTED	SALES INCREASE PAST 5 YEARS	BENEFITS	DEGREE OF SUCCESS
Allentown, Pennsylvania Hamilton Mall	1973	$5,000,000	Semi	4	State and bonds	Renovation of sidewalks and street furnishings	No	Improved street-scape, city image	Somewhat successful
Baltimore, Maryland Oldtown Mall	1976	$2,600,000	Full	2	Urban renewal Community develop-ment	Original form	No	Revitalized blocks, number of businesses increased	Moderately successful
Battle Creek, Michigan Michigan Mall	1975	$2,000,000	Full and semi	4 (1 full 3 semi)	Special assessment and local	Original form	No	Setting for festivals and special events	Not successful
Charlottesville, Virginia Main Street Mall	1976 1976 1980 1985	$4,100,000	Full Full Full Full	8 5 2 1	City capital improve-ments Assessments Federal	Original mall was extended 3 blocks Improved lighting	Yes	Significant increase in retail sales Catalyst	Very successful
Eugene, Oregon City Center Mall	1971	$1,350,000	Full	7.5	Urban renewal City	Reopened one block to traffic Renovated two blocks	No	Improved street-scape image	Neutral
Fresno, California Fulton Mall	1964	$1,600,000	Full	6	Assessment District and urban renewal	No	No	Image pleasant urban space	Moderately successful prior to 1971
Honolulu, Hawaii Fort Street Mall	1969	$2,766,450	Full	6	Private, Board of Water Supply City and County	No	Yes	Retail sales Streetscape	Moderately successful
Ithaca, New York Ithaca Commons	1975	$1,130,000	Full	3	City assess-ments	No	Yes	Helped revitalize downtown Increased property and rental value	Very successful
Lansing, Michigan	1973 1973–1975	$850,000 Lansing Com-munity College	Full Full	3 3	Urban renewal	Yes Three campus blocks on abandoned Washington Avenue	No	Improved physical appearance and brought in new street activities	Moderately successful
Washington Square Mall (North Mall)	1978–1980	South Washing-ton Parking Mall	Semi	4		One way traffic and parking on 3 blocks 2 way traffic one block 1990 opened to traffic on 3 parking mall blocks			

TABLE 8-2 (*Continued*)

LOCATION AND NAME	DATE COMPLETED	COST	TYPE	BLOCK LENGTH	FUNDING TYPES	PHYSICAL CHANGES SINCE CONSTRUCTED	SALES INCREASE PAST 5 YEARS	BENEFITS	DEGREE OF SUCCESS
Napa, California Parkway Mall	1974	$8,000,000	Full and semi	9 (3 full 6 semi)	Federal neighborhood development	Facade upgrades Overhangs added Landscape	No	Catalyst for other development Property values increased	Somewhat successful
New London, Connecticut Captain's Walk	1973	$1,426,209	Full and semi	6 (2½ full mall opened to traffic)	Urban renewal, New London Assoc., state	Completely opened to traffic	No	Image amenities	Not successful
	1991	$1,000,000	Open streetscape						
Ottawa, Ontario, Canada	1967	$636,000	Full	3	Assessment and city	Yes	—	Catalyst for World Exchange Plaza	Moderately successful
Sparks Street Mall	Late 1980's					Complete renovation of mall including paving, street furnishings, fountains		Assessed rental value increased	
Reading, Pennsylvania Penn Square	1975	$1,600,000	Full and semi	2	State, city, assessment County	Some landscaping was removed Additional lights were added	No	Focal point of downtown festivals	Not successful by many but not all
Scranton, Pennsylvania Wyoming Avenue Plaza	1978	$1,000,000	Semi	1	Community development, Economic Development administration and merchants	No	—	Revitalized the block and led to renovation of three additional blocks	Moderately successful
	1983	$2,000,000	Semi	3	Federal Highway Administration	No	—		
Sheboygan, Wisconsin Harbor Center (Plaza 8)	1976	$1,600,000	Full	3½	Urban renewal Local	Traffic was restored and full mall removed	No	Streetscape	Not successful
	1991		Semi now						
Tacoma, Washington Broadway Plaza	1976	$1,500,000	Full Semi now	2	Urban renewal	Limited through traffic, one lane each way with limited parking	No	Helped to revitalize downtown Helped to generate other retail development	Somewhat successful

designed with high quality materials, amenities, adequate seating, areas for gathering, and provide for good maintenance and security.

In the semimall and its streetscape, walk width is important. A 20-foot-wide pedestrian area generally provides room for circulation, sitting areas, and focal points such as sculpture. Fifteen feet should be a minimum desirable width for these areas. On blocks with a 60-foot right-of-way, for example, there can be a 24-foot-wide street and two 18-foot-wide pedestrian areas.

Semimalls have been used in many cities, some of which also have full malls, but they may become more popular because, in effect, they serve as shopping streets that have the benefit of allowing the convenience of the automobile along with wider, better pedestrian areas with quality furnishings and added amenities (see Table 8-2). In several cities such as Tacoma, Washington when automobile traffic was reintroduced, the full mall became a semimall.

SUMMARY

Whichever type of mall is selected, it must be well thought out and approached in providing a quality environment. In cities where full malls have not been as successful as anticipated, these areas should be restudied to see what economic or physical elements need to be changed for success. Simply converting a full mall back to a typical street may not improve business and may be costly if merchandising and other attractions are needed to bring people to the downtown.

The cities in which malls tend to do well are those in which the central business district is a strong core of the overall metropolitan area; many people work and shop there.

3rd Street Promenade, Santa Monica, California.

A reason these cities have strong central business districts is that they often have strong mass transit systems bringing people to a central location. Most of these cities were developed prior to the introduction of the automobile, which tended to pull population out of a single central location. Therefore, most of these older cities also have historical sites and many inner-city residences that further provide a consumer base and add to a mall's success.

In Santa Monica, California a three block full mall was not economically successful after it was built in 1965. To stop further loss of retailing to suburban malls the Rouse Company was selected in 1980 by the city to build a 230,000 square foot enclosed shopping mall called Santa Monica Place at one end of the mall on Third Street. The new shopping center drained business away from the pedestrian mall and caused further decline of the three block area. In

September 1990, the mall called the 3rd Street Promenade was opened to evening traffic with renovation to other street furnishings. Santa Monica Place added some storefronts to face the Promenade, which the shopping mall originally ignored for added visibility. The small shops and some restaurants on the Promenade seem to be surviving and are the backbone of the mall, which is striving to improve its sales.

View of shops added in 1990 in mall area on center island at 3rd Street Promenade, Santa Monica, California.

(preceding pages)

View of marina and
plaza at World
Financial Center,
Battery Park City,
New York.

Ghirardelli Square,
San Francisco.

9

Urban Spaces

This chapter will discuss some particular examples of urban spaces, specifically, festival marketplaces and mixed-use developments. Urban spaces include outdoor public plazas. These plazas are considered to be related to a building or groups of buildings in central city locations. Plazas are gathering places for groups of people of all ages and backgrounds. They are easily accessible and may provide comfortable seating and amenities such as fountains, sculpture, planting; they often have programmed events and food vendors.

Well-designed urban plazas create a sense of place or identity for the downtown. They also have good linkages into adjacent areas. In the United States, plazas have not had the same traditional cultural significance as urban plazas in Europe, where people gather and relax. Examples of some urban plazas are Copley Square in Boston, Paley Park in New York City, Fountain Place in Dallas, and Williams Square, Las Colinas, Irving, Texas. Other types of urban spaces are part of festival marketplaces and mixed-use projects and are discussed throughout this chapter in further detail with some in-depth case studies.

FESTIVAL MARKETPLACES

Festival Marketplaces began in the early 1960s with Ghirardelli Square in San Francisco, California. Festival Marketplaces are retail areas anchored by food and entertainment facilities that are oriented toward office workers at lunchtime, tourists, and the evening and weekend entertainment user. With the development of these marketplaces, added purpose was given to urban spaces and people could dine and shop. The size of these developments in larger cities is often over 200,000 square feet of gross building retail area. Some examples are Faneuil Hall Marketplace in Boston, Massachusetts, Bayside Marketplace in Miami, Florida, and Harborplace in Baltimore, Maryland.

MIXED-USE PROJECTS

Mixed-use projects combine retail uses into the overall developments anchored by office, hotel, residential and/or convention facilities, or other uses. Mixed-use projects often have major pedestrian urban spaces. Some examples of these are Harbour Island in Tampa, Florida and the World Financial Center and Plaza at Battery Park City, New York. Another major new project that has many pedestrian-oriented spaces is Horton Plaza in downtown San Diego, California. This project is a combination downtown shopping center and mixed-use facility with outdoor pedestrian areas.

CASE STUDIES

The following case studies provide examples of various types of urban spaces in the United States, especially related to festival marketplaces and mixed-use developments.

Fountain at Ghirardelli Square, San Francisco.

Faneuil Hall Marketplace

Boston, Massachusetts

Description

Faneuil Hall Marketplace is located on 6.5 acres behind historic Faneuil Hall near the Boston waterfront, between Congress Street and Atlantic Avenue. The initial project included The Quincy Market building containing 75,000 square feet of retail space, the South Market building with 80,000 square feet of retail and 90,000 square feet of office space, and the North Market building with 60,000 square feet of retail and 80,000 square feet of office space. The renovated buildings were completed between 1976 and 1978 and include 70 shops, restaurants, and outdoor plazas with amenities and an ambience related to the historic charac-

ter of the existing buildings and street furnishings. These furnishings include new benches, lighting, banners, shaded sitting areas, and large trees. The architect is BTA (Benjamin Thompson and Associates).

The marketplace cost $42 million with $30 million from private investment and $12 million from public investment.

Development Strategy

In the 1950s the marketplace, originally constructed in 1826, was run down and surrounded by older deteriorated commercial and indus-

trial buildings. This older area also limited access to the waterfront and had a negative impact on the adjacent downtown business district. The city began plans for the waterfront area in 1961. In 1967–1969 the Boston Redevelopment Authority (BRA) began studies on the feasibility of renovating the market. The City of Boston owned the Quincy Market Building, but the North and South buildings, which were privately owned, were purchased through eminent domain. In 1973, the Rouse Company was selected as the developer and manager of the Market buildings by the BRA. Public financing was ap-

Faneuil Hall Marketplace, Boston with its granite and brick paving, outdoor eating areas, and special lighting.

proved for use in development of the Marketplace and the city shares in the overall profits of the project. Federal funds were used for improvements in the project area such as streets and utilities. Annually, Faneuil Hall Marketplace has 90 to 100 million dollars in sales.

Design Features

The outdoor spaces have quality durable materials such as granite and brick paving and unified street furnishings that are harmonious with the nineteenth-century Greek Revival Architecture by Alexander Parrish.

PAVING
The plaza areas are paved with granite slabs unique to the Boston area and brick pavers. The paving reinforces the historic character of the architecture.

LIGHTING
Lights are clear round clusters of globes specially designed for the Marketplace.

PLANTING
Trees are planted in the plaza area and provide shade for sitting areas. Honeylocusts are the type of tree used.

OTHER FURNISHINGS
Other street furnishings include benches, signage, colorful overhead banners, garbage containers, tables with umbrella tops, and features such as a clock.

In Retrospect

Faneuil Hall Marketplace has been very successful with retail sales from its specialty shops, food stores, and restaurants increasing each year. The first year the Marketplace opened 18 percent of the visitors came from outside the area, and by the mid-1980s the figure was over 44 percent. The urban space and marketplace seem to have acted as a catalyst with adjacent areas being revitalized and developments such as Rowe's Wharf only a few blocks away. This has also reinforced the area as a tourist attraction

with the Aquarium, Waterfront Park, Hotel, and other facilities nearby and within easy walk of the central business area.

Faneuil Hall Marketplace also became the model for other similar developments that followed such as Harborplace in Baltimore, Bayside in Miami, Jacksonville Landing in Jacksonville, and South Street Seaport in New York.

View of paving and lighting with clear globes in clusters on metal poles.

Harborplace and the Inner Harbor

Baltimore, Maryland

Description

Harborplace is located on a 3.2-acre site on the northwest end of the Inner Harbor and adjacent to Pratt Street and Light Street. It is also very close to the National Aquarium, which is to the east.

Harborplace is comprised of a group of restaurants and cafes, market shops, small eating places, specialty shops, pushcarts, and kiosks totaling 140 tenants. The development includes two buildings with 247,000 square feet of gross building area and 142,000 square feet of gross leasable area. Harborplace has the amenities of being adjacent to water and open space, easy access to downtown, availability of convenient parking, and the support of the City and its backing of the Inner Harbor area. The pavilions at Harborplace reflect the character and style of wharf buildings that preceded the project. Glass facades were designed that allow the lights and uses of the pavilions to sparkle at night. A two-story height limit was set to keep the buildings beneath the bowsprit of the Constellation, berthed in front of the pavilions. Other amenities include replicas of flags of various shipping lines from the roofs, porticos that allow visitors to see through the structure and that are inviting as entries, brick paving, planting, and sitting areas for the outdoor pedestrian areas.

Development Strategy

Baltimore was founded in 1729 along the historic Inner Harbor of the Chesapeake Bay. In 1904, a great fire leveled Baltimore's downtown financial district, the wholesaling, and dock areas. The fire covered 140 acres and destroyed 1343 buildings. While the area was rebuilt, the Inner Harbor gradually became dormant after World War I. In 1959, the area was considered ready for development and the city and business community began initial downtown revitalization with Charles Center on 33 acres. In 1964, a 30-year program was proposed for the 250 acre Inner Harbor area adjacent to Charles Center.

The main impetus for investment in the Inner Harbor area was the potential for office development. The office building phase from Charles Center had a positive effect on the Inner Harbor area and between 1973 and 1980, five office buildings with 1,650,000 square feet of space plus a federal courthouse and office building were developed.

With the approval of the 30-year plan mentioned above, the Inner Harbor development became a reality and the first stage of the program was to include about 95 acres of land along the three sides of the harbor basin. Public funds included federal grants of $35 million and $17 million in City Bond issues approved by city residents in 1966 and 1982. Beginning in 1968 a heavy duty bulkhead and a promenade were constructed around the basin. The U.S. Frigate Constellation, the oldest warship of the U.S. Navy, became the focus of the harbor in 1972.

The Rouse Company made a proposal to the city in 1977 for the Harborplace site. In February 1978 the Baltimore City Council gave approval to the Harborplace design concept. A city referendum was petitioned, voted on, and received approval in November 1978. Harborplace had a tight construction schedule and was opened on July 2, 1980. The architect was BTA.

Design Features

The buildings echo the wharf buildings that were formerly on the site. Separate and distinct character was designed for each of the two structures, which have exposed concrete structure and lightweight steel frame and roof. Outside walls are predominantly glass.

PROMENADE

A wide plaza area for strolling and sitting paved with brick circles the harbor linking various facilities. This pedestrian area has street furnishings, sculpture, sitting areas, night lighting, kiosks, and other amenities.

BENCHES

The benches are made of wood.

PLANTING

Trees are planted along parts of the plaza promenade.

NIGHT LIGHTING

The lights are cube shaped with five on black poles along the Harbor edge of the promenade. Single luminaires are are used in other locations.

BOLLARDS

Nautical elements are located along the promenade and give a special character to the edge treatment.

SCULPTURE AND FOUNTAINS

There is a large sculpture adjacent to the Maryland Science Center that one can walk under and a fountain adjacent to the pavilions.

In Retrospect

Harborplace was built by private investors. The project provided $3 million dollars in taxes during the

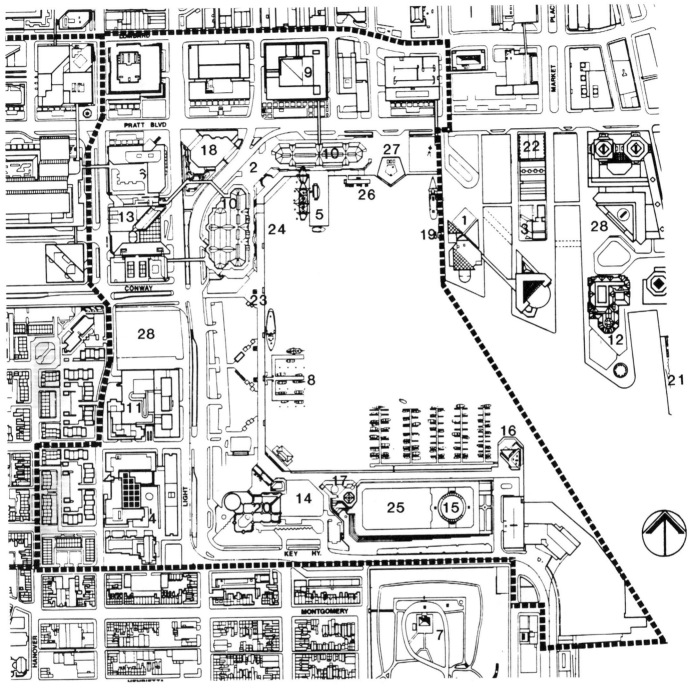

1. AQUARIUM
2. CEREMONIAL LANDING, SKIPJACK MINNIE V
3. CHART HOUSE RESTAURANT
4. CHRIST CHURCH HARBOR APARTMENTS
5. CONSTELLATION DOCK U.S. FRIGATE CONSTELLATION
   HARBOR TOURS & EXCURSIONS
   CRUISE BOAT LANDING
6. CONSTELLATION PLACE & SHOPS
7. FEDERAL HILL
8. FINGER PIERS
9. GALLERY AT HARBORPLACE
10. HARBORPLACE
11. HARBOR COURT HOTEL, APARTMENTS & SHOPS
12. HARRISON'S PIER 5 AND LIGHTHOUSE
13. HYATT REGENCY HOTEL & RESTAURANT
14. INNER HARBOR CAROUSEL
15. INNER HARBOR FLOWER GARDEN
16. INNER HARBOR MARINA & RUSTY SCUPPER RESTAURANT

17. INTERNATIONAL PAVILION & PLAY SCULPTURE
18. McKELDIN SQUARE
19. MARITIME MUSEUM, SUBMARINE TORSK
    & LIGHTSHIP CHESAPEAKE
20. MARYLAND SCIENCE CENTER & IMAX THEATRE
21. PIER 6 CONCERT PAVILION
22. POWER PLANT
23. PROMENADE
24. PUBLIC WHARF (VISITING SHIPS)
25. RASH FIELD
26. SMALL BOAT RENTALS
27. WORLD TRADE CENTER & OBSERVATION DECK
28. PUBLIC PARKING

Plan of Baltimore Inner Harbor.
(Courtesy of Center City-Inner Harbor Development, Inc.)

View of Harbor-
place with Con-
stellation docked in
Harbor.

View of amphi-
theatre area with
brick paving at
Harborplace.

View of Harbor-place with outdoor eating areas.

View of promenade and streetscape elements.

first year of operation. The number of jobs provided, estimated at 1000, has turned into 2500 because of the success of the development. An estimated 33 percent of the visitors reside outside the metropolitan Baltimore area. Harborplace also helped generate publicity for the Inner Harbor, which has become a popular gathering area on the east coast. Other attractions include the National Aquarium, Inner Harbor Marina, Maryland Science Center, World Trade Center, Constellation Dock, U.S. Frigate Constellation, Pier 6 Concert Pavilion, Public Works Museum and Streetscapes, restaurants, and other facilities.

Of greatest importance to the Inner Harbor were the following four major projects completed between 1977 and 1981: the Convention Center in 1979, Harborplace in 1980, the Aquarium in the summer of 1981, and the Hyatt Regency Baltimore Hotel in October 1981.

Bayside Marketplace

Miami, Florida

Description

Bayside Marketplace is located on a 22-acre site including open space along Biscayne Bay in Miami, Florida. Bayside also connects with the 208 slip Miami Marina. The development comprises two sets of parallel pavilions that are adjacent to the edge of the marina with an open air area at the bend or turning point between the north and south pavilions. Two smaller pavilions are on either side of an entry plaza, which leads to the urban plaza adjacent to the marina. There is also an octagonal restaurant building and a 1200 car parking garage. Bayside has 310,000 square feet of gross building area with 235,000 square feet of gross leaseable area and 172 tenants.

The architecture by BTA is an expression of the subtropical climate and materials indigenous to the area. This along with bright colored awnings, flags, and other furnishings give the development a regional character quite different from Faneuil Hall Marketplace and Harborplace.

Development Strategy

Bayside Marketplace, which was completed in 1978, is the focus of the city's restoration of the 60-acre Bayfront Park. The development is a civic improvement built on land that was once underwater. Bayside established 1200 jobs and carried an official mandate for minority participation. When Bayside opened 77 minority merchants had leased space. First year total sales reached $72 million, a little less than anticipated. Sales per square foot average $400 with half of the merchants at $500 per square foot.

The City of Miami receives rent based on sales performance. The minimum rent was $325,000 for the first year.

Design Features

The marketplace pavilions have shed roofs, shutters, open verandas, and breezeways. Tree shaded walkways, fountains, and colorful awnings, flags, and accent materials provide an exciting atmosphere for the project.

View of entrance to Bayside.

View of open
pavilions and
vendor's kiosks
near entrance.

View of open
pavilions.

View of pavilions from marina.

View of pavilions with sitting and observation area.

245

PAVING

Red brick pavers with concrete edge bands are used throughout the development. In addition, along areas overlooking the marina, boardwalk areas are provided.

LIGHTING

Lights along walk and plaza areas have hoods that are connected to metal poles that curve down to connect to the hoods.

SEATING

Benches are provided along plaza areas and there are also some movable chairs in some locations.

FOUNTAINS

In a few spaces fountains are provided as a focus. The fountains are made of masonry.

OTHER FURNISHINGS

Flags and awnings are also provided, which lend a colorful atmosphere to Bayside.

PLANTING

Palm trees and other subtropical plant material lend an indigenous quality to this project.

In Retrospect

Bayside creates a sense of place in Miami. It provides a unique area that brings every major ethnic group into a community facility. Bayside created 1200 jobs for the Miami area. It was set up with a mandate to have minority participation, and it opened with 49 percent minority merchants leasing space. The pavilions, which have open-air facilities, provide open verandas, breezeways, and awnings. They also create shopping streets and spaces that have a sense of ambience.

Other facilities at Bayside include an amphitheater at Bayside Park that opened in the spring of 1988 and Miami's new sports arena. Bayside is also close to Miami's rapid transit system, which loops around the downtown. The overall development has been successful with Bayside generating sales of $400 to $500 per square foot.

Walk area, seating, and lighting with a canopy of palm trees.

Fountain as focal
element with
potted plants in
foreground.

Covered sitting
area with awnings
adjacent to
pavilions.

World Financial Center, World Financial Center Plaza, World Financial Center Winter Garden, The Esplanade, and South Cove Park

Battery Park City, New York

Description

Battery Park City is located on a 92-acre site adjacent to the Hudson River to the West and the West Side Highway to the East. The World Financial Center completed by architect Cesar Pelli in 1988 creates a new impressive addition to the New York skyline. The height of the buildings ranges from 9 to 51 stories for the tallest tower. The commercial area is also linked to the World Trade Center to the east by pedestrian bridges.

The World Financial center Plaza and the World Financial Center Winter Garden are part of the commercial center. The landscape architects for the project were M. Paul Friedberg and the artists for the plaza were Scott Burton and Siah Armajani.

The commercial area has retail facilities with shops and restaurants. Six million square feet of commercial office space is provided in four buildings that subdue the adjacent World Trade Center with its 110-story towers.

The Winter Garden faces the plaza and the Hudson River to the west. It is a 130-feet-high barrel vaulted space that is also connected to the World Trade Center by a pedestrian bridge. The plaza level of the space is open with adjacent enclosed areas with shops and restaurants. The space has 18,000 square feet and is planted with

a bosque in rows of four 30-foot Mexican Washington Palms. Paving is marble in an intricate pattern designed by Pelli's office.

Development Strategy

Battery Park City is located on a 92-acre landfill along the Hudson River. The Battery Park City Authority was created in 1968 to develop the landfill, which was partly created by excavated material from the World Trade Center. Although several plans were developed for the area none seemed to link adequately with the adjacent areas. In 1979, the Authority leadership changed and was con-

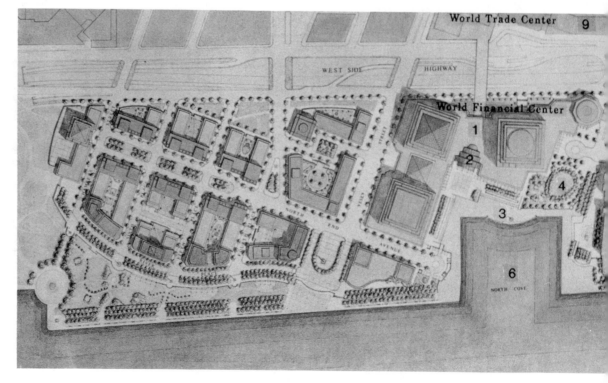

Plan of Battery Park City with World Financial Center. (Plan by Cooper, Eckstut Associates). Key: (1) World Financial Center, (2) World Financial Center Winter Garden, (3) World Financial Center Plaza, (4) Pump House Plaza, (5) The Esplanade, (6) North Cove, (7) South Cove, (8) South Cove Park.

View across marina area toward World Financial Center Winter Garden.

nected to the Urban Development Corporation. The firm of Cooper, Eckstut Associates was selected to prepare a new master plan. The master plan called for 6 million square feet of office space, 14,000 housing units, and 30 percent open space in parks, plazas, and an esplanade.

The firm extended Manhattan's street system into the development area and provided an esplanade along the river. A set of architectural guidelines was also developed that called for use of materials that would harmonize with the city's present fabric and set requirements for building sizes and shapes, location of lobby entrances, dimensions of sidewalks, etc. The guidelines were enforced by the Authority during the various phases of the development.

The World Financial Center Plaza

The plaza is located on 3½ acres along the Hudson River and provides an exciting setting with its marina where large sail boats and yachts are moored. The plaza was a collaborative effort of the building architect, landscape architect, and two artists. It has several specialized areas. Outdoor cafe dining areas are close to the office buildings. These are buffered from major pedestrian circulation by rows of trees and a linear fountain with a water wall. Stepped terrace areas lead to the main plaza area where granite benches in seating areas look out to views of the marina and Hudson River. The plaza is paved with granite pavers.

The Esplanade

The Esplanade is a 1¼ mile promenade along the Hudson River. It links the North Cove area with the World Financial Center and the South Cove, with its linear 3-acre park along the waterfront.

The Esplanade provides a place for residents, visitors, and workers and is both a park and a walkway. The landscape architects for the project are Hanna/Olin, Ltd. The designers researched the city's traditional street furnishings and World's Fair benches, hexagonal asphalt pavers used in New York Parks are used. A granite seawall and curved iron railing with a revised type of Central Park's lighting fixtures punctuate the railing and are

Interior view of Winter Garden.

World Financial Center Plaza with Battery Park City Lights and granite seating area overlooking the marina.

Fountain with waterwall and outdoor restaurant area above on upper terrace. Granite pavers are used on the plaza.

Stepped walking and sitting areas between main plaza and upper terrace.

Pump House Plaza area with sitting areas and planting using clump birch.

Wooden benches
used in Pump
House Plaza area.

The Esplanade with
hexagonal asphalt
pavers, Battery Park
City Lights, and
wood and iron
benches.

Concrete and wood
benches typical of
New York City area
are used along The
Esplanade.

Sitting area with
tables for playing
checkers or chess.

placed on raised portions of the granite wall.

Trees used on the promenade include an allee of silver lindens along the upper walkway. Japanese Pagoda trees are adjacent to the promenade closer to the river. Beds of shrubbery, grasses, and flowers are also used.

A sculpture called the Upper Room by artist Ned Smyth is located along the Esplanade at Albany Street. It is placed on a 40 × 70 foot raised platform enclosed by columns and is made of pink concrete.

South Cove

The South Cove area is a 3-acre park that looks out toward the Statue of Liberty. The design of the park in-

cluded reshaping of the cove's edge, sculpting topography, and the use of indigenous plant material. The project was designed in collaborative effort by landscape architect Child Associates, Inc., Stan Eckstut Associates, and artist Mary Miss.

Features include a lower promenade along the cove's edge with a wooden jetty at the end of South Cove. There is also a curved boardwalk, a viewing platform with a steel circular stairway, and a variety of lighting fixtures from victorian to art deco styles.

In Retrospect

The World Financial Center Plaza is a dynamic space with areas for outdoor dining, relaxing, and viewing the

yachts in the marina or sitting adjacent to the linear fountains with their water walls. The plaza connects to the promenade, which is a major pedestrian promenade that is successful with its well-designed street furnishings, where people can stroll, ride bicycles, and view the Hudson River. The promenade connects to the South Cove area where the 3-acre park has viewing areas toward the Statue of Liberty.

The World Financial Center Plaza, which only recently opened in 1988, forms an impressive public open space with a variety of uses reminiscent of European spaces. The buildings that define the space gradually shift from a stone skin at the base to glass at the top, visually lightening

Sculpture called the Upper Room by artist Ned Smyth is located on The Esplanade at link with Albany Street.

the buildings as they rise upward. The towers also, by the use of different heights, create a series of steps, relating the development to the areas beyond as a part of the composition. The overall project has become a landmark in urban design. It has provided a new way of approaching architecture with the street and urban open space providing structure for buildings.

Residential areas were developed on the north side and south side of the commercial area. North area guidelines follow standards developed for the south area, which includes Rector Place, a 9-acre area with 2000-unit residential complex surrounding a 2-acre park. The four block development has 12 parcels to attract a variety of private developers.

The original strategy for the housing areas was to provide one-third luxury housing units, one-third moderate income units, and one-third subsidized units. The financial crisis of the late 1970s made that unworkable, but funds were committed to units in other parts of the city. These funds were provided from Battery Park Cities revenue and the first $400 million has already been committed.

Wooden walk area along South Cove area with a variety of lighting fixtures.

Horton Plaza

San Diego, California

Description

Horton Plaza is a mixed-use regional shopping center located on an 11.5-acre site in downtown San Diego in a nine block area defined by Broadway and G streets and First and Fourth Avenue.

Horton Plaza, opened in 1985, combines elements of both a festival mall and a conventional shopping center. The architect for the project is Jon Jerde. The development by the Hahn Company has four department stores for 482,000 square feet of gross leaseable area (GLA). Total GLA is 885,000 square feet. The gross building area is 1,161,000 square feet. The development also has 2350 structured parking spaces.

It is an open air, vertically stacked mall with a serpentine pedestrian walkway. Although the anchor stores are located in the corners, there are five levels with pedestrian walkways guiding one by landmark features, bridges, stairways, and escalators. The development also includes restaurants, fast food, gourmet market, specialty shops, packaged food, and movie theatres.

Walkway leading up an interesting stairway at the Mercado with brick paving on the plaza area.

Development Strategy

In 1871, Alonzo Horton gave a block of land in front of his hotel for a public park, "Horton Plaza." Previously he had purchased 960 acres of what is presently downtown San Diego.

Redevelopment began in 1969 with an initial redevelopment area of three blocks and improvement of Horton Plaza Park. An organization of business leaders, San Diegans, Inc., lobbied the city to plan a larger area around the park, and, in 1972, the city council approved a redevelopment plan for a 15-block Horton Plaza plan. The plan along with a market study

became the impetus for a major competition to develop the land. The Hahn Company was selected to negotiate with the city in 1975. For the next 7 years the development firm negotiated with prospective retail anchors for the project.

City Council also created the Centre City Development Corporation (CCDC) to act as sole negotiator between the city and developers. In October 1982 when the four anchors committed to the Hahn Company, it obtained private financing and the land acquired by the CCDC was conveyed. Groundbreaking took place shortly thereafter.

Design Features

Horton Plaza was influenced by Southern Mediterranean marketplaces. Staggered shop levels were developed on both sides of the paseo with four levels on the northeast corner and five levels on the southwest due to the site's 35-foot change in height. A 40-foot-wide one-way service tunnel acts as a fire lane and provides access to nine separate loading docks with their own freight elevators. Entrances to Horton Plaza were carefully located and linked to the existing street pattern.

View of major circulation area showing various levels at Horton Plaza and the type of atmosphere, which is very dynamic visually.

PAVING
Paving is mostly concrete with some special areas of brick.

LIGHTING
Fixtures with round white globes light the open spaces.

FURNISHINGS
There are a variety of sitting areas. Some have movable tables and chairs. Other elements include a clock tower, and three sculptures. The sculptures are an obelisk by Joan Brown, a 60-foot curved teak "prow" by Loren Madsen hanging above the entry court of the Mercado, and a "light clock" by Peter Alexander.

PLANTING
Planting is placed in specific areas such as the Mercado, and used as an accent.

Street furnishings such as a clock tower are used.

259

In Retrospect

During its first year, Horton Plaza performed in the upper 10 percent of the Hahn Company shopping centers. The center has created about 2000 permanent jobs. Downtown activity has increased with the Lyceum Theatre and 7-screen movie theater. Over 170 hours of free entertainment are scheduled each month.

Validated parking is used at Horton Plaza with 2 hours of free parking for shopping with a validated ticket and longer for the movie theaters. The project links to the Omni Hotel to the west and is adjacent to the Wells Fargo Bank Building and Spreckels Building to the north on Broadway. Horton Plaza is an exciting place to visit, buy lunch, and shop.

Pedestrian bridges linking various areas.

Harbour Island

Tampa, Florida

Description

Harbour Island is located just south of downtown Tampa's business district on a 177-acre site previously known as Seddon Island. The site once separated from the downtown by Garrison Channel is now linked by an elevated light rapid transit line plus the Franklin Street Bridge.

The overall mixed-use development designed by the Hillier Group in conjunction with Design Arts Group, Inc. will eventually have 1,000,000 square feet of office space, 240,000 square feet of specialty retail and restaurants,

900 hotel and conference rooms, and 4650 residential condominiums with covered parking for each use.

Phase I of the development, which opened in 1985, has a nine-story class A 196,000 square foot office building and a 300-room continental style luxury Wyndham Harbour Island Hotel oriented toward traveling businessmen and small to medium sized conventions.

The retail space called The Shops on Harbour Island has a 66,434-square foot gallery of specialty retail shops, express eateries, and sit down restaurants. There are approximately

50 shops and restaurants. The shops originally planned as a festival market have waterfront exposure with brick plazas, fountains, a promenade, and small amphitheatre. Also, Phase I has 550 condominium residences and a 44-slip marina to add atmosphere to the project. A series of villages are included in Phase I, the first residential community called Seddon Cove has 72 units of 1500 to 2300 square feet in four waterfront buildings and range in price from $235,000 to more than $400,000. Harbour Court will have 128 units starting at $99,000 and ranging to $174,000 in two seven-

This light rapid transit line connects Harbour Island with downtown Tampa.

View of entrance
treatment at drop-
off for shops and
hotel.

View of festival
market building
and plaza adjacent
to Tampa Bay.

story mid-rise buildings. Harbour Homes, which are townhomes, are priced from $140,000 to $224,000. They were designed by The Benedict Group. There are also 29 single-family Island Homes ranging in price from $490,000 to $655,000. The architects for these homes is The Architectural Design Consultants and Bloodgood & Associates.

An athletic club provides approximately 34,000 square feet for sports activities. Seventeen clay courts and one hard court are available including a grand slam stadium for professional tournaments. A 25-meter outdoor pool, racquetball and squash courts, basketball court, and fitness rooms are also part of the club facilities.

Development Strategy

Harbour Island, a few hundred yards from downtown Tampa in Tampa Bay, had a lot of potential being so close to the downtown. In 1973, Major Realty of Orlando bought an option on the island and developed plans that got nowhere. Another developer, Oscar E. Dooley, picked up the option in 1976, and came up with a Disney type of amusement center that never materialized, but in 1979 Beneficial Corporation bought the island for $3

million. Under a joint agreement with Lincoln Property Company, for 5 years the Dallas Developer built, leased, and managed the project through April 1986. It then reverted back to the Beneficial Corporation, which in 1987 developed an agreement with Trammell Crow Residential, which is currently developing both Harbour Homes and Island Homes.

Design Features

The mixed-use development has the concept of an old world festive market. Archways, balconies, and canopies on the building facades create focal points and a distinctive character. Brick is used throughout the development and is complemented by bronze glass and copper standing seam roofs.

PLAZA PAVING
The plaza is paved in brick with one area along the bay stepping down with concrete steps to form an amphitheater.

SEATING AREAS
There are some seating areas on the plaza and in the food court inside the building.

PLANTING
Palm trees and other planting adds interest to the plaza areas and at the entrance to the hotel and office buildings.

LIGHTING
Round white globe type luminaires are used in plaza areas. The fixtures have three globes.

FOUNTAIN
The focus of the amphitheater area along the bay is a fountain out in the bay with a high jet of water.

OTHER ELEMENTS
The marina with its slips adds much to the atmosphere of the project. There are also directories, and special signage. In addition the housing units have a New York-style of urban environment with a density of 15 units per acre.

In Retrospect

Phase I of Harbour Island is well underway with the 300-room hotel, Shops on Harbour Island retail area, an office building, condominiums, an athletic club, and apartments. The total buildout is planned for a 10- to

View of outdoor eating area adjacent to food court.

263

15-year period with about a $1 billion dollar investment.

Harbour Island was planned to be a strong enough draw to attract patrons for the Shops and related facilities with 66,000 square feet of retail area. When the retail area first opened it was referred to as a festival market because of the food court and shops. It was found that the Shops on Harbour Island did not have enough space for the facilities needed to attract enough users. Many other festival markets have about 200,000 square feet of floor space. Also, the other festival markets are located in larger cities with much larger numbers of downtown workers to draw from, particularly at lunchtime. Tampa's downtown workers number only about 30,000 and the downtown was never a retail hub.

The Shops on Harbour Island did not have adequate impact to be immediately successful, and it also could have been planned with a stronger theme incorporated with uses such as restaurants, bars, and theaters. The opening of the Tampa Convention Center just across Garrison's Channel in October 1990 has substantially improved sales, with about a 25 percent increase. At present occupancy is

Marina facilities for boats are provided to add atmosphere to the project.

over 90 percent. In the near future other facilities in Tampa should help to attract more people onto Harbour Island. A downtown aquarium is anticipated and cruise ships have begun docking adjacent to the Island. Two cruise ships began visiting recently and the third will begin in December 1991.

Although initially the development failed to attract enough people, there is beginning to be noticeable improvement. In a sense the project was ahead of its time. The outdoor spaces with cafes and a view of the Convention Center provide a unique area for residents and visitors.

Also, because of its location and accessibility Harbour Island has become Tampa's downtown park. Harbour Island had a concert and fireworks in 1991 for Memorial Day with a backdrop of Her Majesty's Yacht Britannia, which was docked at the Island. On the 4th of July, Freedom Fest 1991 featured music and fireworks. At buildout the permanent nonconstruction jobs to be created by Harbour Island are 5300 with projected annual tax revenues from the total development of $28,684,830.

Residential units are part of the mixed-use project which will eventually have 4650 condominium units and covered parking.

Bibliography

Alexander, Laurence A., *Downtown Malls, An Annual Review*, Volume 2, New York, Downtown Research and Development Center, 1976.

Aschman, Frederick T., "Nicollet Mall: Civic Cooperation to Preserve Downtown's Vitality," *Planners Notebook*, September 1971.

Bacon, Edmund N., *Design of Cities*, New York, Viking, 1974.

Bernatzky, Aloys, "Climatic Influences of Greens and City Planning," *Anthos*, No. 1, 1966.

Bernatzky, Aloys, "The Performance and Value of Trees," *Anthos*, No. 1, 1969.

Carpenter, Philip L., Theodore D. Walker, and Frederick O. Lanphear, *Plants in the Landscape*, San Francisco, W. H. Freeman and Company, 1975.

Carr, Stephen, Ashley/Myer/Smith, *City Signs and Lights*, for Boston Redevelopment Authority, Cambridge, M.I.T. Press, 1973.

Chamberlain, Gary M., "Bring New Vitality to Main Street," *The American City*, November 1969.

Darlow, Arthur E., "Miami to Upgrade the Downtown," *The American City*, August 1959.

Eimon, Pan Dodd, "The City Tells Its Story," *The American City*, November 1960.

Elliott, C. H., "Long-Term Benefits of a Shoppers' Mall," *The American City*, March 1964.

Faull, Harry A., "Pomona Sets a Pattern," *The American City*, January 1964.

Fruin, John J., *Pedestrian Planning and Design*, New York, Metropolitan Association of Urban Designers and Environmental Planners, Inc., 1977.

Goldstein, Jan/Bassuk/Lindsey/Urban, "From the Ground Down," *Landscape Architecture*, January 1991.

Gruen, Victor, *Centers for the Urban Environment*, New York, Van Nostrand Reinhold Company, 1973.

Haimback, David, "The Fresno Mall," *The American City*, April 1965.

Hajdu, J. G., "Pedestrian Malls in West Germany: Perceptions of Their Role and Stages in Their Development," *Journal of the American Planning Association*, Summer 1988.

Hibschman, Robert A., "Downtown Pedestrian Shopping Malls," Planning and Development Department, City of Eugene, Oregon, September 1989.

Houston, Lawrence O., "From Street to Mall and Back Again," *Planning*, June 1990.

Howell, Richard L., "The Untapped Urban Resource," *Parks and Recreation*, September 1975.

Kemmerer, Harleigh, "Managing Outdoor Lighting," *Grounds Maintenance*, 1976.

Knack, Ruth E., "Pedestrian Malls: Twenty Years Later," *Economic Development Commentary*, Summer 1984.

Kozel, P. C., "Superior Trees for Landscaping," *Landscape Industry*, February/March 1975.

Lynch, Kevin, *The Image of the City*, Cambridge, M.I.T. Press, 1960.

Malt, Harold L., *Furnishing the City*, New York, McGraw-Hill Book Company, 1970.

Martin, Roger, "Exciting Start with Nicollet Mall," *Landscape Architecture*, July 1969.

Nelson, Carl, "How Main St., Evansville, Came Alive," *The American City*, November 1973.

Newton, Norman T., *Design on the Land*, Cambridge, Massachusetts, Belknap Press of Harvard University Press, 1971.

Redstone, Louis G., *The New Downtowns: Rebuilding Business Districts*, New York, McGraw-Hill Book Company, 1976.

Robinette, Gary O., *Plants/People/and Environmental Quality*, Washington, D.C., U.S. Department of the Interior, National Park Service, in collaboration with the American Society of Landscape Architects Foundation, 1972.

Robinette, Margaret A., *Outdoor Sculpture: Object and Environment*, New York, Whitney Library of Design, 1976.

Rouse, James, "Festival Market Places: Bringing New Life to the Center City," *Economic Development Commentary*, Summer 1984.

Rubenstein, Harvey M., *Central City Malls*, New York, John Wiley and Sons, 1978.

Rubenstein, Harvey M., *A Guide To Site and Environmental Planning*, 3rd Ed., New York, John Wiley and Sons, 1987.

Schlivek, Louis B., "Four Places Where Urban Design and Planning Are Paying Dividends," *A.I.A. Journal*, August 1975.

Spreiregan, Paul D., *The Architecture of Towns and Cities*, New York, McGraw-Hill Book Company, 1965.

ULI, "Bayside Marketplace, Miami, Florida," *ULI Project Database File*, 1987.

Weisbrod, Glen, and Henry O. Pollakowski, "Effects of Downtown Improvement Projects on Retail Activity," *Journal of the American Planning Association*, Spring 1984.

Williams, Alva, Jr., "Free Parking in Downtown? You're Kidding!" *Traffic Engineering*, June 1975.

Winslow, Joan, "Semimall Brings Shoppers Back to Town," *The American City*, February 1974.

Wyman, Donald, *Trees for American Gardens*, New York, The Macmillan Company, 1990.

Zion, Robert L., *Trees for Architecture and the Landscape*, New York, Reinhold Publishing Corporation, 1968.

Index